# *Raymond Queneau*

## Twayne's World Authors Series
### French Literature

David O'Connell, Editor
*University of Illinois*

TWAS 763

# Raymond Queneau

## By Allen Thiher

*University of Missouri*

*Twayne Publishers* • *Boston*

*Raymond Queneau*

Allen Thiher

Copyright © 1985 by G. K. Hall & Company
All Rights Reserved
Published by Twayne Publishers
A Division of G. K. Hall & Company
70 Lincoln Street
Boston, Massachusetts 02111

Book Production by Lyda E. Kuth
Book Design by Barbara Anderson

Printed on permanent/durable acid-free
paper and bound in the United States of
America.

**Library of Congress Cataloging in Publication Data**

Thiher, Allen, 1941–
   Raymond Queneau.

(Twayne's world authors series; TWAS 763. French literature)
   Bibliography: p. 140
   Includes index.
1. Queneau, Raymond, 1903–1976—Criticism and
interpretation.   I. Title.   II. Series: Twayne's world
authors series : TWAS 763.   III. Series: Twayne's world
authors series.   French literature.
PQ2633.U43Z93   1985        843'.912        85-7606
ISBN 0-8057-6613-8 (alk. paper)

# Contents

# About the Author

Allen Thiher is professor of French at the University of Missouri in Columbia. He completed his Ph.D. in 1968 at the University of Wisconsin after spending a year in Paris as a Fulbright Scholar. He has also written *Céline: The Novel as Delirium* (1972), *The Cinematic Muse* (1979), and *Words in Reflection: Modern Language Theory and Postmodern Fiction* (1984). He was a Guggenheim Fellow in 1976–77 and has published work in such journals as *philological Quarterly*, *PMLA*, *boundary 2*, *Dada/Surrealism*, *Film/Literature Quarterly*, *Kentucky Romance Quarterly*, *Modern Fiction Studies*, the *French Review*, and the *Journal of Literary Theory*.

# *Preface*

In this introductory study of Raymond Queneau I hope to accomplish two objectives: to offer some acquaintance with Queneau's major literary works and to lay bare some of the centers of coherence through which these works generate meaning. I stress "literary works," since Queneau's total work encompasses an extraordinary number of fields, including philosophy, mathematics, historiography, and criticism, as well as creative works in the normal sense of the term. Minor literary works have also been omitted from consideration, and the reader will find only such reference to his nonliterary works as throw light on Queneau's poems and novels. This choice is not arbitrary, however; for Queneau is primarily, in the broadest sense, a poet, and the interest we may take in his ideas about history, science, or language is largely derivative from our concern with the quite central place that his major literary works occupy in the history of modern French letters.

This volume may also be seen, implicitly at least, as an argument in favor of the latter claim. Until recently Queneau's audience has been restricted to a fairly small group of cognoscenti and enthusiasts, though these have included such readers as Roland Barthes, Boris Vian, Alain Robbe-Grillet, Eugène Ionesco, Italo Calvino, and Georges Pérec. In his *Exercises in Style* and *Zazie in the Metro* Queneau had two best-sellers; but by and large he has been a writer's writer, a model both by example and by the enormous energy he brought to the public practice of writing. The range of his intellectual activities was also an impressive model for emulation, for it is no exaggeration to claim that Queneau had at his disposal more knowledge in more fields than virtually any other modern writer. The range of knowledge he could muster in defense of literature, and especially in promulgating an antiromantic aesthetics, made him a formidable pedagogue for two generations of French writers.

Queneau's use of all the idiomatic resources of French has meant that, with the exception of a few Italian and German writers well versed in French, nearly no writers outside of France have been receptive to his influence. In this volume, moreover, it is presupposed that my readers have little or no knowledge of French, which has imposed a slight limitation. I have not put as much emphasis on Queneau's wordplay in French as might be expected. However, there is an advantage to be gained here, since this strategy has allowed me to assume that Queneau can be translated; and that his linguistic experimentation presupposes larger structures of meaning that are accessible in translation. I would argue, moreover, that his word games take on their full meaning only when they are situated within these structures of meaning. I hope that this study will facilitate access to those structures composing Queneau's literary universe. Readers equipped with enough French to follow Queneau's play with his native language can then find several studies, in French, that can guide them in greater detail into Queneau's word-play and purely verbal creation.

Central to my understanding of Queneau's play with language and literary structures have been notions of transgression, parody, and festive or carnivalesque travesty. For insight into these concepts I express my indebtedness to the great Russian critic Mikhail Bakhtin, whose *Rabelais and His World* has been singularly useful. Many of the parodistic devices and forms of travesty found in Rabelais recur in Queneau. This is not altogether surprising. Queneau saw in Rabelais one of his literary forebears, and in many ways he is our modern Rabelais. With regard to other debts, among the several useful studies of Queneau's work that one might consult perhaps the most useful for the beginning reader is Claude Simonnet's *Queneau déchiffré (Notes sur "Le Chiendent")*. More than notes on Queneau's first novel, *Le Chiendent,* this work is an introduction to Queneau's literary universe, and I would like my own book on Queneau to be considered as complementing Simonnet's masterful study.

Finally, I would like to acknowledge my gratitude to the University of Missouri for the research leave that has facilitated the preparation of this study. I would also like to thank the Research Council of the University of Missouri for the travel grants that have made it possible to undertake research in the Bibliothèque nationale in Paris. Thanks must also go to André Blavier, Claude Debon, and David O'Connell for their various forms of help, as well as to Wanda Elbert and Linda Dowell, those stalwarts in the Department of Romance Languages at UMC who keep scholarship flowing.

Allen Thiher

*University of Missouri, Columbia*

# Chronology

1947    *Exercises de style. On est toujours trop bon avec les femmes* published as pulp paperback under pseudonym of Sally Mara. *Bucoliques,* collection of poems.

1948    *Gueule de Pierre* and *Les Temps mêlés* revised and published together as *Saint Glinglin.*

1950    *Petite cosmogonie portative,* poem; *Bâtons, chiffres et lettres,* collection of essays. *Journal intime* under pseudonym of Sally Mara.

1951    Elected to the Goncourt Academy.

1952    *Le Dimanche de la vie,* novel. *Les Ziaux* and *L'Instant fatal,* with some other poems, appear as *Si tu t'imagines.*

1955    Member of jury at the Cannes Film Festival.

1956    *Présentation de l'encyclopédie de la Pléiade,* announces his goals as editor of this encyclopedia. *Pour une bibliothèque idéale,* literary survey. Screenwriter for Bunuel's film *La Mort en ce jardin.*

1958    *Sonnets* and *Le Chien à la mandoline.*

1959    *Zazie dans le Métro,* novel, his first best-seller.

1960    Foundation with François Le Lionnais of the Ouvroir de littérature potentielle or Oulipo.

1961    *Cent mille milliards de poèmes.*

1962    *Entretiens avec George Charbonnier,* interviews.

1963    *Bords,* writings on and around mathematics and philosophy.

1965    *Les Fleurs bleues,* novel.

1966    *Une Histoire modèle,* a model for the study of history.

1967    *Courir les rues,* first volume of trilogy of poems.

1968    *Le Vol d'Icare,* novel; *Battre la campagne,* second volume of trilogy of poems.

1969    *Fendre les flots,* final volume of trilogy of poems.

1973    *Le Voyage en Grèce,* selection of essays and reviews written primarily in the thirties.

1975    *Morale élémentaire,* final "cosmology."

1976    Queneau dies on 25 October.

1977    Foundation of Les Amis de Valentin Brû, an associ-
        ation devoted to Queneau's work.

1981    *Contes et propos* brings together nearly all of Queneau's
        stories, short pieces, etc.

1982    Creation by André Blavier of a Centre de Documen-
        tation for Queneau studies in Belgium.

# Chapter One
# Queneau:
# The Life of the Mind

The briefest biographical résumé of the life of Raymond Queneau could read that he was born in 1903 in the port of Le Havre, came to Paris in 1920 to study philosophy, and spent the rest of his life there, involved in virtually all the intellectual and creative currents of his time until his death in 1976. He married, had a son, and was fond of such normal human activities as drinking; but in a very real sense his life was his work, and vice versa. Virtually every important event in his life took the form of an encounter with books and ideas, or with the creators of those books and ideas that shaped the artistic, intellectual, and scientific milieu in Paris and, more generally, of our time. If Paris was a movable feast, as Hemingway called it, it was especially a feasting place for men and women hungry for ideas and creative adventures, for new plastic forms and revolutionary concepts. Queneau was such a creative reveler; he was a nearly perfect representative of that unique French specimen, the independent intellectual who lives for the fête that ideas can offer the playful mind.

Queneau once claimed that his earliest memory of Le Havre was of the days of popular joy, of the *liesse* that existed during Carnival, before World War I, when people paraded beneath the balcony of his parents' apartment.[1] Queneau was enough of a devotee of Freud to know that this memory could well be a fantasy, but nonetheless more significant than any "real" memory, especially for a writer whose work unfolds as a carnivalesque celebration of language. Quite different from this memory is the misery Queneau seems to have known as a child and which, in a psychoanalytic perspective, he portrays in his major poem, *Chêne et chien*. Queneau recognized that he had a certain saturnine temperament that caused him to interpret things always in the worst light, and his contradictory attitudes toward childhood must be seen in the perspective of this ambivalence. On the one hand, he often wanted to recover the innocence

1

and joy of childhood (and even said that he had never left childhood); on the other hand, he usually viewed his childhood as a time of unredeemed misery and anguish. It does seem that he had some fun, discovering the popular language of comic books, going to silent movies, and reading and writing from his earliest age. These discoveries were as important for his later writing as his drawn-out Oedipal complex.

Queneau came to Paris in 1920, and his parents moved to a Paris suburb where they owned, by what one can judge from a photograph, a rather comfortable bourgeois home. Equally as important as his studies for a *licence* in philosophy were the friends he made among the surrealist poets, such as André Breton, Paul Eluard, and Louis Aragon. Queneau soon rejected surrealist goals, and had a personal dispute with André Breton (though they later seem to have become friends again). But there can be no doubt that surrealism was one of Queneau's most important encounters. Not only did his first published texts appear in the review *La Révolution surréaliste,* but, more importantly, surrealism established a climate of ludic exper-imentation in which literature could be viewed as a form of play. The surrealist interest in dreams, in psychoanalysis, in madness and occult thought, as well as "heteroclite" systems, remained with Queneau throughout his life. Queneau took himself to be a rebel during his youth, though his rebellion was as much motivated by his asthma attacks or by his discovery of political injustice as by a desire to transform human existence through the liberation of eros, as the surrealists wanted. The novel *Odile* portrays how estranged Queneau probably was by the surrealists' irrationalism. Even if his skepticism was doubled by an almost religious need for redemption, the skeptic in Queneau could never take seriously the impossible goals surrealism gave itself for liberating man from his fallen rational state.

Surrealism provided Queneau with an education he could not get at the University of Paris, and he remained friends throughout his life with most of the surrealists, including Breton, and the dissident surrealists, such as Jacques Prévert, Michel Leiris, and André Masson. After surrealism—and James Joyce's *Ulysses*—Queneau's most important encounters were with the work of the German philosopher Hegel, psychoanalysis, and mathematics, though not necessarily in that order. Queneau studied mathematics from childhood and was reading Boutroux, Borel, and Cantor while at the university. Freud was utilized by the surrealists to underwrite their program for liberating desire; and Queneau underwent several years of psychoanalysis during the thirties. Queneau's attitude toward psychoanalytic theory is ambiguous. If he recognized the therapeutic value of sessions on the doctor's couch, he was also skeptical about how those sessions might be used and was profoundly ambivalent about the nature of the unconscious. Queneau wrote hardly a work that does not contain some reference to psychoanalysis, often in a parodistic vein that shows he was as much attracted to it as repelled by it.

Hegel looms so large on Queneau's horizon that one could say that much of Queneau's work is a meditation on Hegel's grand failure. Hegel was little read in the French university during the twenties, though Queneau apparently was reading him during his military service during 1925–27.[2] With his friend Georges Bataille he attended the lectures on Hegel that Alexandre Kojève gave during the thirties (and which Queneau edited and published in 1947). Hegel had theorized that with his philosophy absolute mind had come to consciousness of itself, and, therefore, history had come to an end. For history is the record of the development of mind's consciousness of itself in time. There is a circular logic to Hegel's claim to have ended history, and Queneau was more than a little attracted to it. One could claim that at least half the time Queneau believed but little in history, and Hegel's claim to have ended it coincided paradoxically with Queneau's own disbelief in the possibility of history. In any case, history is a leitmotiv in Queneau's work that often presupposes Hegel's grand system of history's necessary development as the background against which Queneau's fabulations or lamentations must be read.

The thirties saw other encounters. Queneau spent time during the early part of the decade in the Bibliothèque nationale doing research on *fous littéraires*. The project entailed gathering enormous quantities of long quotations from literary and scientific madmen of the nineteenth century. Queneau's obsession with "heteroclite thought" resulted in the compilation of an *Encyclopédie des sciences inexactes*. No one wanted to publish this encyclopedia (at least until André Blavier completed it), but Queneau did make use of it in his novel *Les Enfants du Limon.* He also attended courses by Puech on gnosticism and Manichaeism, those heretical versions of early Christianity whose visions of man's fall unceasingly fascinated Queneau.

In 1963 Queneau wrote an essay on Georges Bataille in which
he said that at the beginning of the thirties they read together not
only works on Hegel, Husserl, and the first translation of Heidegger
in French, but also works by Marx and Engels. At this time Queneau
was a politically concerned writer who joined Bataille in writing for
the left-wing *La Critique sociale,* a publication of the Cercle com-
muniste démocratique directed by the anti-Stalinist Boris Souvarine.
Many of these reviews and essays, from this periodical and others,
have appeared in *Bâtons, chiffres et lettres, Bords,* and *Le Voyage en
Grèce.* They show what a satirical polemist Queneau was and what
a virtuoso he was in a number of fields, ranging from literature and
anthropology to science and politics. Especially in the essays published in *Volontés* in the later years of the thirties, Queneau appears
ready to engage combat on two primary questions, the nature of
knowledge and poetics.[3] He is resolutely skeptical of any exaggerated
claims for science and is even more hostile toward any poetics that
make inspiration or the unconscious the key to poetic revelation.
Queneau's attacks on surrealism in *Volontés* are a defense of classicism,
or Queneau's belief in rational lucidity as the basis for creation.

Another polemical subject on which Queneau spent much energy
in the thirties and into the fifties was the question of the necessity
of reforming French literary language. In Queneau's view written
French had become a dead language and could again be a living
literary language only if its syntax and spelling were reformed. This
reform should draw upon the resources of popular spoken French,
with its living syntax and vocabulary, as well as find spelling that
would respect phonetic reality. Critics have often made much of
this polemic to explain the liberties Queneau takes with written
language. In my view, however, Queneau's views of language seem
somewhat outmoded today. His acceptance of the primacy of spoken
over written language can hardly be granted the status of an axiom;
and, as Queneau knew, any phonetic representation of spoken language is ultimately quite arbitrary. His theoretical views on language often bear only a tangential relation to the linguistic
inventiveness and verbal transgressions that characterize his writing,
a writing distinguished by a willingness to play with all the forms
of written as well as spoken language. His supposed transcriptions
of spoken language are, moreover, usually forms of transgression
against literary correctness that depend on a recognition of the codes
of written language for their aesthetic effect. In any case, Queneau

recognized late in life that his polemic had had no effect and was not really to the point as a description of the evolution of French.[4]

In 1932 Queneau made a trip to Greece and, according to one version of the story, used popular language to write his first novel, *Le Chiendent (The Bark Tree)*, after he noted the great distance between written Greek and the demotic or spoken language.[5] Supposedly, in this first novel Queneau set out to translate Descartes's *Discourse on Method* into popular French. *The Bark Tree* is a very Cartesian novel, but Queneau later said that he had actually intended on this trip to translate *An Experiment in Time* by John Dunn, a writer who more or less used relativity theory to show that we have memory of future events.[6] In any event, we have here a good example of Queneau's eclecticism, for, not only was he reading Descartes and Dunn, but also Faulkner and Kierkegaard as he began to write a novel in which parodies of Plato, Parmenides, Hegel, and Heidegger are in the service of a Joycean demonstration of the possibilities of fiction. In spite of this, or because of it, *The Bark Tree* was not a best-seller.

Gallimard published Queneau's first novel, and in 1938 he went to work for this editor as an English language reader for the *Nouvelle Revue Française*. War came two years later, and Queneau spent the "phony war" in a small provincial town where he did little except talk and drink copious quantities of red wine, at least according to a comic essay he wrote on hoodlums and philosophers.[7] Another source suggests he also read Plato and Montaigne.[8] He returned to Paris, apparently barely escaped deportation, and continued throughout the Occupation his many activities as writer, editor, and journalist. He also began frequenting what we might call the new Saint-Germain-des-Prés generation of existentialists, including Jean-Paul Sartre, Simone de Beauvoir, and the writer on whom he had a marked influence, Boris Vian. Existentialism designates a philosophical current that draws upon Heidegger and Nietzsche, with roots in Kierkegaard and Hegel. Queneau cannot in any strict sense be called an existentialist, though many of his attitudes and concerns parallel those of Sartre or Camus. Certainly some of his novels and poems published at this time, say *Pierrot, Loin de Rueil (The Skin of Dreams)* and *L'Instant fatal,* are the expression of a sensibility that is in tune with the dominant absurdist thought that characterizes French existentialism. In good dialectical fashion Queneau was never hesitant to parody the central concepts of existen-

tialism, even if many of the tenets of existentialism are in harmony
with some aspects of his own outlook.

After the war Queneau began to acquire a literary reputation,
partly because of the great success of his *Exercices de style (Exercises
in Style)* of 1947, partly because of the extraordinary range of his
activities in many areas. Friend of everyone from Henry Miller to
Miro, Queneau signed numerous petitions, was a member of many
juries and committees, worked in film, translated works, appeared
on the radio, became known as the author of a hit song, and was
involved in a prodigious number of other projects. Central to all
this activity was a commitment to promoting, in an often disin-
terested way, the life of art, literature, and knowledge, for Queneau
seemed tireless when it came to defending culture.

There is often a pedagogical side to all this activity. Consider in
this respect *Pour une bibliothèque idéale* (For an ideal library), a survey
sent in 1956 to a good many writers in which they listed their
choice of the great books. Such a list makes impossible demands
that were certain to please Queneau, which probably explains why
he, who detested questionnaires, accepted to edit it. In his own
contribution he begins by complaining that such a list is necessarily
incomplete if it does not list the classics of mathematics, Newton,
Einstein, Neumann's *Theory of Games,* or Bailly's Greek dictionary,
to name a few included omissions. Queneau then proceeds to give
a list that includes not only the expected classics of Greek, French,
and world literature; the major works of Western philosophy; and
the great modernists such as Joyce and Kafka; but also the comic
books of his youth, Gertrude Stein, and a long list of Oriental
writers and books: the *I Ching,* Confucius, Taoist thinkers, poets
such as Li Po and Tu Fu, and a number of Japanese writers, especially
the diarists. Queneau clearly wanted to educate his readers and to
suggest that the canon of great books must be expanded to include
those Oriental writers whose culture is at least as rich as our own.
And for Queneau's readers this list shows another, ongoing encounter
that they must be aware of if they are to enter fully into Queneau's
literary creation. Oriental literature is a part of Queneau's rich
intertextual universe.

In 1950 Queneau joined the Collège de Pataphysique. This "college" is dedicated to the pursuit of the science of pataphysics, a
creation of the early twentieth-century writer Alfred Jarry. Pataphysics is the science of imaginary solutions; or alternately, the

science of the particular, not the general. Therefore, it is the science of the absurd, which could only appeal to the skeptical Queneau, whose distrust of systems of any sort grew as he matured. As his *Petite cosmogonie portative* and other writings show, Queneau stayed abreast of scientific research, and his doubts were founded on good acquaintance with science. His adherence to the ironic lunacies of pataphysics was in part an outgrowth of his recognition of the limits of science. For Queneau came to see science as a kind of game that allowed the mathematical formalization of relationships, but which could offer no knowledge of things in themselves. As he put it in an essay on mathematics in classification in science, scientists play games not unlike chess or bridge, in which all one "knows" is a method that the community of scientists accepts as valid.[9] As scientists of the absurd, the community of pataphysicians promotes multiple games, publishing with ironic malice and satiric logic such studies as Queneau's essay on the aerodynamic properties of addition. Pataphysics is a science to which Lewis Carroll could have subscribed.

As befits a pataphysician Queneau was never afraid of contradictions, and shortly after joining the college he undertook another project that, in his own eyes, was an impossibility. He agreed to edit the multivolume encyclopedia of the Editions de la Pléïade. Ever since childhood, when he wrote a catalog for his library, Queneau had been obsessed with the desire to find systems for organizing knowledge (he wrote, after all, three prefaces to *Bouvard et Pécuchet,* Flaubert's novel on the impossibility of systematic knowledge). With this editing task Queneau saw himself, with his usual classical sense of continuity, as a continuer of an encyclopedic tradition that went back at least to the Assyrian king Ashurbanipal and for which his immediate forebears were Bacon, d'Alembert, Ampère, Comte, and Dewey. In his presentation of the encyclopedia in 1956 Queneau offered a kind of manifesto that perhaps best characterized his attitude toward knowledge and its possibilities: "Nowhere in this undertaking will be hidden the dimensions of our uncertainties and the immense quantities of our nonknowledge. The reader will learn not to know, and to doubt. This is also a critical undertaking. The principal benefit of scientific method is lucidity."[10] This passage throws light not only on what Queneau saw to be the benefit of scientific activity, but of all intellectual activity, including that pataphysical formalization of the particular, literature.

Mathematics and pataphysics have a number of affinities, since both are games that allow one to pose arbitrary axioms and then to work out the conclusions that follow. Queneau's attitude toward mathematics varied throughout his life, and if the alter ego in *Odile* is a Platonist in his belief that mathematics reveals a world that exists in itself, the Queneau who wrote an essay on the German mathematician Hilbert seems to have accepted that mathematics is essentially a formalism that works through the internal consistency of its definitions—something of the reverse mirror image of pataphysics.[11] This interest in mathematics and literature led Queneau in 1960 to join with his mathematician friend François Le Lionnais to found a "subgroup" within the Collège de Pataphysique. This group took the name of the Ouvroir de littérature potentielle or Oulipo. Dedicated to inventing new literary forms or renewing the use of old ones, this group met and meets frequently in public sessions. The genesis of "potential literature" is conceived by these players to be a public, and often quite festive series of games, from which all trace of anguish before the blank page is banished. Their usual practice is to set forth some explicit constraints, game rules often of a mathematical nature, and to generate texts that obey the rules they have established in advance.[12]

Oulipo practices can involve the mathematical transformation of existing texts, which often generates a kind of mechanical parody; or they can impose precise constraints for the writing of new works, much as has traditionally been the case for the writing of poetry throughout the history of literature. Oulipo thus combines experimental writing with a neoclassical sense of the history of literary forms considered as quantified rules for performance. One might call this practice avant-garde neoclassicism: avant-garde in its attempt to find new models for literary creation, neoclassical in its concern to make the rules of writing a matter of public knowledge and verification. Such a paradoxical formulation would also describe much of Queneau's work. Oulipo rejects, moreover, the romantic and surrealist aesthetics that Queneau had attacked in the thirties; for nothing could be further removed from an attempt to harness inspiration or to explore the unconscious than the creation of these public games that frankly acknowledge their provisional nature and their rational game mechanisms. It is not surprising that Queneau was one of the most assiduous "workers" at the monthly luncheons of Oulipo.

Despite all his public activities Queneau continued to produce poems and novels on a regular basis until he died in 1976. Queneau was a public figure most of his life; yet it is difficult to evaluate him as a man during the last decades of his life. If he was a willing participant in many public forums, he was the most modest of men and refused consistently in interviews and conversations to speak about himself and his private life. This modesty was no pose. Queneau was an antiromantic who saw no reason to make a public figure of himself as a man. Writing, creation, and ideas were, on the other hand, public concerns on which he would discourse willingly. The life of the mind was, for Queneau, a great ludic activity that perforce had to have a public dimension.

Queneau's reserve is of course one of his most important personal characteristics. It sprang from a fundamental attitude about the life of the mind and the private life. His friends and associates often attribute Queneau's modesty to the kind of skeptical wisdom that he came to embody, not unlike an Oriental sage. We do know that he was quite affected by his wife's death in 1972; and it appears that his journal, at some distant publication date, may contain some surprising revelations about his personal beliefs—although, given his dialectical skepticism, it is hard to imagine what he could have believed at any given moment that could surprise us. In any event, Queneau's career embraces most of what has been of real interest in French letters and intellectual life in the twentieth century. From the life of the mind that he unceasingly cultivated sprang a body of work that is one of the richest produced in France, or in any other country, in modern times; it is to these poems and novels that we shall now address ourselves.

# Chapter Two
# Surrealism and Beyond: The Early Poetic Texts

In his essay on the fauvist painter Vlaminck, Queneau wrote the following lines that tell the importance he attributed to the appearances of the world:

It is rather strange after all to paint landscapes. It is clear that in them it is always a question of man. The universal landscape is the earthly paradise. It is from there that one always paints, from paradise, whether it be situated behind or before you, after the fall or before redemption.
Every landscape painting is an apocalypse, since we know well that we do not live in the earthly paradise. Nature itself has compassion for the miserable and driven *(traquée)* life of man. A suburban wall, a plane tree by the road, a shop sign in the wind, a black puddle of snow, a trolley that squeals, and one recognizes all the tragedies of humanity.[1]

Queneau, long a painter himself, accepted that there are no privileged subjects for art. Every appearance, every object, every image, and every word can enter into art's experiencing of the world, for the world is nothing except this totality. Yet, Queneau uses the Christian myth of paradise and the fall to situate this world. And if Queneau was a skeptic about the possibility of knowing any religious truth, he nonetheless knew that his sensibility was molded by a tradition and a culture. He accepted that the only possibility for speaking about the world was to accept that culture and the possibility for discourse that it offered. Sometimes this acceptance takes the form of parody; at others, as in his comments on the painter's assumption of the fall, Queneau is a poet of tragic lamentation.

Queneau found his voice as a poet first in association with the surrealists, a group hardly known for their acceptance of man's fall. Queneau's earliest poetic texts show that he annexed the surrealist revolt to his own black vision of man's fall. As a young poet Queneau

found in the surrealist revolt against the limits of human existence
an analogue to his own lamentation about the fallen nature of human
institutions and, ultimately, all of creation. There can be little doubt
that Queneau's own physical suffering, especially from asthma, motivated in part his early nihilistic vision of existence, but his revolt
against creation in his early poems goes far beyond merely denouncing pain and physical misery. Existence is corrupted from within,
and as fundamental as suffering are the tendencies toward dissolution
and the overwhelming boredom that characterize man's destiny: his
lot is entropy and ennui. One can understand the attraction surrealism exercised on Queneau, since its less than modest program
aimed at radically transforming the conditions of existence (and
perhaps a trace of surrealism remains in Queneau's contention that
every painting is an apocalypse). But one can also understand that
Queneau was something less than a surrealist at heart, since their
radically optimistic belief in the possibilities of transforming man,
of "living poetry," could not really be shared by a pessimist like
Queneau.

Queneau was marked by melancholy from his youth and was
equally receptive, one might argue, to that Jansenist strain of pes-
simism that has colored French culture since the seventeenth century. Jansenism's radical vision of human incapacity and decline is
one of the most perduring themes of French culture, even when
divorced from its strictly Christian context. In this sense Queneau,
like Flaubert, Céline, and Sartre, accepted a worldview that was at
once nihilistic and based on the structures of an originally religious
experience that saw the world as a locus of fall and of predestined
degeneracy. Such a worldview explains why Queneau, often with
self-directed irony, was attracted to Gnostic and Manichaean religious thought. These religious doctrines, early heretical versions of
Christianity, squarely emphasized that the world is a place without
light and that time itself is the essence of evil. For a nocturnal poet,
like Queneau, suffering in mind and body, such visions of total evil
had undoubtedly an almost comic capacity for offering solace for
the unredeemed fall of existence from whatever early paradise one
might dream about.

Queneau did, however, have his surrealist phase, and one should
not underestimate its importance for his poetic practice. The reader
who turns to *Les Ziaux* (1943) or *L'Instant fatal* (1946) encounters
poems going back to at least 1920, and many of them are works

that embody both surrealistic themes of revolt and the procedures of surrealist rhetoric. Moreover, Queneau's first published texts appeared in the surrealist publication *La Révolution surréaliste* in the late twenties and show to what an extent Queneau, until his break with André Breton, was attempting to begin his career as a writer under the banner of surrealist revolt.

I stress this surrealist phase in Queneau's career, not only because he chose to publish some of his surrealist pieces in *Les Ziaux* and especially in *L'Instant fatal,* but also because the surrealist texts point to certain basic configurations that recur throughout Queneau's work. For example, "Le Tour de l'ivoire"—whose title literally means "the ivory's turn," but suggests a play on "ivory tower"— is an exemplary expression of negative revolt. First published in *La Révolution surréaliste* in 1927 but included in *L'Instant fatal,* this poem conveys a strong sense of Queneau's revulsion before the injustice of human institutions and the inevitability of man's fall.[2] Justice is likened to a bird of prey, weighing upon the nuptial chambers in which might take place the revolution in eros that surrealism demanded. Queneau may have only briefly subscribed to the surrealist belief that eros could lead to a transformation of existence, but he remained true enough to his own vision of injustice to publish this text again after World War II. "Le Tour de l'ivoire" enacts a surrealist overcoming of man's fall, and this is a basic configuration for Queneau's work throughout his career. His poems and novel repeatedly attempt to overcome man's penchant for happiness, explicitly in Queneau's earliest works, and implicitly in the later texts, through his final *Morale élémentaire.*

Queneau's other surrealist texts, it should be noted, do not usually propose a surrealist vision of the liberation of desire. This is true of the poems published in *Les Ziaux* and *L'Instant fatal* as well as the few other pieces that appeared in *La Révolution surréaliste.* For example, one finds another example of Queneau's rage in his "Texte surréaliste," published in 1928. Although this angry text sets forth two surrealist allegories about love, it focuses on *ennui,* a form of "fulgurating anguish." And, in one of the earliest of Queneau's many considerations about the nature of the unconscious, this piece declares, in contradistinction to what many surrealists held, that the unconscious is "despair and unhappiness." The unconscious can be likened to "trees that grow without noise for fear of frightening the woodcutters, fish that swim in silence, crystals that accumulate without anything betraying their development, the hand of a clock that one cannot see leaping, afraid, over the bristling of seconds. . ."[3] The unconscious is presented as a fearful realm of disordered images, a kind of nothingness, and yet a place where "medusas prepare their attenuated silence and the idea of evil crosses the zone defended by two haggard will-o'-the-whisps." Medusas and other forms of aquatic life are an image throughout Queneau for what is other, and this nonhuman alterity takes on, in this surrealist text, a hallucinatory and disquieting appearance.

In another poem of the twenties, Queneau could ironically note that Freud's "Traumbedeutung mange les chimères," that is, that the *Interpretation of Dreams* feeds on strange fantasies, but these fantasies are also sources of anguish and distress in many of Queneau's early texts.[4] In the "Texte surréaliste," for instance, the poet prefers to flee these fantasies by escaping into a night that is at once an image of dissolution, or disappearance, and is in its primordial darkness closer to the fundamental nothingness than is the light of day. Morning only reveals the disgusting daily trivia that the young surrealist Queneau, in his revolt, cannot abide: "the coherent notary, the sordid priest, the housewife who buys fruit made rotten by the merchant's breath, the filthy cop with his filthy nose . . ." (14).

It is also noteworthy that in his "Texte surréaliste" Queneau gives himself over, in the creation of two surrealist allegories about love, to a play with words, to deforming the material form of the linguistic signifier, that is a trademark of much of Queneau's writing. The allegories themselves are exercises in incongruity. One tells of the love of a capricorn, perhaps in the sense of a capricorn beetle, for "a lava"; and the other allegory narrates the love of a certain Edgar for a woman-isthmus. A sign of the zodiac that can also be an insect offers a play of possibilities for "reading" love both as destiny and as an animal. This is a conceptual game. In the second allegory Queneau takes the material body of the word as the body of love. For the isthmus, as a word and as a lover, is mutilated when a stranger appears and bends the letter *i* into an *a*, leaving in French *asthme* (asthma) where there had been *isthme* (isthmus). The word-lover is then decapitated, leaving only the French phoneme *thme*, which in turn permutates into "ténia [tape worm], tendon, tension, tenseur, censeur [censor]" (16). That the material form of the word should transform itself into *asthma*—and into what Queneau sees as asthenia or pathological weakness—shows the poet's distrust of

the physical body, the body of love and of language, for the material
body bears the weight of man's fall and all his suffering. Yet, the
poet is drawn to the game possibilities inherent in the various
associations that are condensed in the material signifier. One could
see here, without undue exaggeration, Freud's earliest influence on
Queneau's poetic practice, for there is a parallel here with the rhetoric
of dream interpretation that insists on the multiple meanings, often
contradictory, that can be condensed into a single symbol or signifier. But Queneau's play with condensation is also quite self-
conscious, and points to the way he dislocates language for subversive
or transgressive purposes.

Queneau wrote poems throughout the twenties and thirties, but,
with the exception of the few texts appearing in surrealist sources,
he published virtually none of them. Queneau's readers in the thirties
therefore knew him primarily as a novelist until he published in
1937 the long poem *Chêne et chien* (Oak and dog) which he rather
puckishly called a novel in verse. But *Chêne et chien* is clearly a poem,
one of the major poems written in French in the twentieth century,
and in many respects the key text for entering into Queneau's literary
universe. Drawing upon his experience of several years of psychoanalysis, the poem sets forth what one might call Queneau's personal
mythology. It attempts in addition to overcome the myths that
have condemned him to unhappiness by presenting a festive redemption of existence.

*Chêne et chien* is divided into three numbered parts. Each of these
parts is divided into a number of sections without title or number
(though in an effort to guide the reader in this discussion I shall
refer to individual sections of parts 1 and 2 in terms of their nu-
merical order of presentation). The first part relates episodes from
Queneau's childhood. The second tells of his analysis, but also sets
forth the solar symbolism that Queneau offers as a personal cosmology or a countermythology to psychoanalysis. This part also
explains the sense of "oak and dog" as his personal emblems for the
opposing drives that rend him. The third part, entitled "The Village
Festival," celebrates a triumphant fête, or the festive impulse that
Queneau seemingly offers as an alternative to psychoanalysis and an
analytical approach to creating the conditions of happiness. *Chêne
et chien* replicates the structure of the poem "Le Tour de l'ivoire" in
that it proposes a triumph over the conditions of unhappiness, but
it does so by proposing a festive victory over the unconscious that

Freudian analysis would lay bare. In a sense the third part proposes a Rabelaisian celebration as a way of overcoming the ontology of decadence that one finds throughout the poems Queneau was writing in the twenties and thirties (and which he was apparently able to publish only after writing *Chêne et chien*). In brief, one might say that in *Chêne et chien* Queneau is writing an anti–*Waste Land;* drawing like T.S. Eliot upon the resources of modern psychology and anthropology to describe a condition of sterility and destruction, Queneau sets himself squarely against the American writer by proposing joy as the only remedy for our fall into modernity.

Queneau marks the distance that now separates him from surrealism by beginning the work with a quotation from a letter by Boileau stating that he tries to write what has not yet been said in French. As the seventeenth-century poet who was the very embodiment of the classical rationalism that the surrealists wished to subvert, Boileau signals at the outset of *Chêne et chien* Queneau's intent to respect tradition, or, rather, to incorporate tradition into his own poetic practice. Throughout the poem Queneau uses traditional verse forms, alexandrines and octosyllabic verse, with various rhymes and assonances. These forms, however, seem to clash, especially at the poem's beginning, with a diction that seems contrived in its banality:

> Je nacquis au Havre un vingt et un février
> en mil neuf cent et trois
> Ma mère était mercière et mon père mercier:
> ils trépignaient de joie.[5]

> I was born in Le Havre on a twenty-first of February
> in nineteen hundred and three
> My mother was a haberdasher and my father too:
> they jumped for joy.

Queneau begins with the most quotidian diction to narrate a kind of autobiography composed of memory fragments. As the poem develops, these fragments take on increasingly the character of fetishistic memories, obsessional images of the sort that would readily flow forth on the psychoanalyst's sofa. In effect, the poem's first part predicates a kind of psychoanalytically oriented listener who hears the poet begin at the beginning of his life and then continue, first chronologically, then by association, as he recalls painful memories, images of unhappiness, sexual themes, and bodily motifs, all associated with his fall into unhappiness.

Queneau's very birth is a form of fall. As he presents it, from his early separation from his parents when he was sent to a wet nurse, his birth condemned him to the fallen world of the petty bourgeoisie. For the child it was a world of vile odors and disgusting sensations, of dirt and sweat, a world of daily labor whose only result was wasted investments in stocks and bonds that proved worthless in the economic reverses that took place in the early twentieth century. Queneau's reference to historical events, such as the loss of value of the bonds his parents bought, points to how he sees his own personal fall imbricating those historical moments that make up that decadence known as "universal history." Such a view of history sheds light on why Queneau, throughout his life, saw the overcoming of history to be as much a necessity as triumphing over his inborn desire for unhappiness.

The difficulty of mastering one's own personal history is reflected in the poem's discontinuous fragmentation. The first narrative movement of the work runs quickly from Queneau's birth to his sexual initiation in a brothel. But the past that the poet would narrate refuses linear arrangement; it fragments into diverse narrative lines that could result in infinite complications; and strict chronology must give way to discontinuity. Thus he relives in the present a scene where he "is" five, a child militarist playing at burning toy soldiers with a prism; or he describes himself "picking his nose" in school while learning writing, reading, and arithmetic. Other scenes are narrated in the past. He recalls the secondary school and his terrorized fascination with buttocks, especially those of the school teacher's son when she would whip him; and those of his mother in the toilette. Images of flesh, in all its less flattering aspects, abound as testimony to a perpetual presence of the body's decadence and the disgust it excited in the child.

Parents are of course at the center of the child's world, and Queneau speculates, in good Freudian fashion, on how he may have wished their death. Associated with this wish are other terrors: a deformed dwarf, hoodlums that preyed upon the children, or some form of "sorcerer" who extorted money with the threat of making Queneau's mother die. The childhood portrayed by *Chêne et chien* is quite different from the romantic and surrealist visions of childhood as a magic realm in which the child can participate, through the power of his imagination, in an ecstatic world that defies the limits of adult rationality. Queneau's childhood unfolds in a fearful realm in which the full measure of creation is given by its failure to grant the child any magic powers. Yet there is a trace of innocence that the poet cannot forget: "et je m'éffrayais du mélange / de l'ordure et de l'innocence / que présentait la Création" (and I was terrified by the mixture / of filth and innocence / that Creation offered, 37). The poet clearly needs to find a principle of innocence in a world in which one is guilty, as any Jansenist would have known, for no other reason than for having been born.

Queneau can find little innocence in the first part of his poem; rather he is more fascinated with "singular objects" wherein "vibrated the demonomanie of corruption" (45). He finds, moreover, that he had a certain taste for "filth and muck," for hatred and despair, and all this is symbolized by a maternal image that offers little solace: "le soleil maternel est un excrément noir" (the maternal sun is a black excrement, 45). But this child nonetheless desires the excremental mother who is "unfaithful" to him, and, in almost textbook fashion, Queneau's Oedipal revolt against his father ends with his being beaten.

Queneau recognizes his complicity in his taste for unhappiness, he recognizes his capacity for rationalizing and accepting the "little castration" (48) that he can then blame for his incapacity to accept adult life. From this kind of rationalization may have sprung Queneau's obsession with numerology, a mania that characterized Queneau throughout his life. For numbers, in their apparent objectivity, offer a kind of rationale or justification for phenomena. In *Chêne et chien,* for example, he discovers that at the age of thirteen he has already acquired a personal history, just as nations acquire a public identity: "Treize est un nombre impair / qui préside aux essais de sauver l'existence / en naviguant dans les enfers" (Thirteen is an odd number / that presides over attempts to save existence / by navigating the underworld, 57). Thirteen remained one of Queneau's favored "explanatory" numbers and is inscribed in often arcane ways throughout his work. But even at thirteen the destructive child looked back upon the darkness of childhood and ultimately found only shadows, "caverns and cellars, anguish and penitence" (58).

For the past really seems to elude any apprehension, either at the moment of the poem's creation or in the past itself as the child

meditated on his earlier life. Night and dissolution menace all, and
the poet doubts that he can seize the "true meaning" of his "so-
called memories"—*prétendus souvenirs* (58). Queneau admits to finding only fog and shadows there where he searches for his own life.
In the first part of the poem the recovery of the past is seemingly
impossible.

The first part of *Chêne et chien* does not end on this note of failure,
however; for there is one clear trace of the past that speaks in the
present. This is the voice that addresses itself to the poet in the
final section of the first part, the voice of the third-person pronoun
*on:* " 'Tu étais' / me dit-on 'méchant, / tu pleurnichais avec malice
/ devant des gens de connaissance / c'était vraiment très embêtant
. . .' " ("You were," they say, "bad, / you whined out of spite/ in
front of people we knew/ it was very embarrassing . . .," 59). Here
speaks a voice that is still alive for the poet: the internalized voice
of the other that chides him, in the present, for his moral deficiencies
in the past. In this last section direct discourse, taking the form of
the inquisitorial voice, speaks a past and can lead directly to the
second part of the poem with its explicit portrayal of psychoanalysis.
It is this inquisitorial voice, crippling the child-poet by telling him
that everything he does is idiotic, that analysis must attempt to
master.

Queneau draws upon another seventeenth-century writer, the English mystical poet Thomas Traherne, for the epigraph to the poem's
second part: "To Infancy, o Lord, again I come / That I my Manhood
may improve." A possible irony is found here in Queneau's choice
of lines from a rather obscure religious poet to preface his own lines
dealing with psychoanalysis, which might suggest by implication
that Freud could be likened to a mystical poet. But Traherne's lines
can also be taken literally, for they do describe the psychoanalytic
project: to bring the neurotic to a recognition of conflicts rooted in
his childhood. With this recognition the analyst can hope to effect
a purgation, acceptance, or transfer of the conflict that will finally
improve the patient's manhood.

The second part of *Chêne et chien* is divided into nine sections, of
varying length, that vary freely in metric schemes. The first section,
for example, plays with free verse to present a rather ironic vision
of the hapless patient's plight:

je suis incapable de travailler
bref dans notre société
je suis un désadaptaté inadapté
né-
vrosé
un impuissant
alors sur un divan
me voilà donc en train de conter l'emploi de mon temps

I'm incapable of working
in short in our society
I'm an unadapted disadaptated
neu-
rotic
an impotent
so here on a divan
I'm telling the way I spend my time

(64)

The forced repetition of the rhyme using the vowel *é* and the comic neologism *désadaptaté* warn the reader that Queneau is not going to offer him a standard version of the interpretation of dreams. The first dream he tells leads to a proliferation of interpretative possibilities, as do the endless number of dreams that he could possibly tell.

In the first dream he describes, he sees himself as a crocodile, "docile as a dog," following a man and woman along a river. This image of docility conflicts with his image of himself as a rebel, a surrealist with left-wing beliefs. The paradox resolves itself when he realizes that his rebellion demands in turn that he punish himself for revolting against the paternal authority figure: "mon père agonisant gorgé de maladies / et mon amour / qui doit être puni / mon amour et mon innocence / mon amour et ma patrie / mon amour est ma souffrance / mon amour est mon paradis / *le vert paradis des amours*" (my father dying stuffed with diseases / and my love / that must be punished / my love and my innocence / my love and my fatherland / my love is my suffering / my love is my paradise / *the green paradise of loves,* 65). These lines express the paradoxical dilemma of the neurotic who loves his father and yet revolts against him, and therefore must be punished for this love that is apparently associated with the father's dying. At the same time, this love of the child and parent provides the only image of paradise that the poet can imagine, but paradise is forever lost. The final line, taken from Baudelaire's "Moesta et Errabunda," makes an ironic intertextual homage to the poet who wanted as much as any writer to believe in the lost paradise of childhood, and more than any other found that childhood was paradise only because it was lost. Suffering and paradise are inextricably bound up as the two sides of the fall.

Baudelaire is not the only poet cited for his attempt to find again the paradise of childhood. In the second section Mallarmé's "Don du poëme" ("Gift of the Poem") is parodied for its portrayal of creation as a kind of birth. Mallarmé as priest-creator brings forth in his creation a "child of an Idumean night." Queneau finds his task decidedly less noble, for in *Chêne et chien* he must content himself with bringing forth a poor child of a bituminoid (or tarred) night, a sullied child of darkness.

The central motif of the second part's second section is given by the image of fishing. A boat on the sea, surrounded by floaters indicating the nets beneath the surface, give a metaphor for the psychoanalytic quest and its attempt to dredge up from the depths the repressed memories that, like so many fish, can be laid out to the light of day. In lines that are not altogether clear, Queneau seems to find only sterility and death in this fishing (spaces are "boned," plains cleared, and turtles die in their shells); and in what appears to be a direct address to the doctor the poet tells him that "his dreams" are drier than herrings' tails; that poetry is dead; and that mystery gives off a death rattle (65–66). For the doctor has reduced the "other reality"—perhaps the surreality of poetry—to a mere question of the poet's relation to his parents at his youngest age.

This indictment of psychoanalysis continues in the second part's third section, for it might appear that analysis prevents the poet from speaking. The poet gives a long negative litany of all the things—grass, oaks, sand, stars, and dogs—about which he had nothing to say at this point. Yet each stanza in this negative list also notes the presence of sounds, of a humming, a breathing, a murmuring, a spasm, that seem to inhabit the poet or the space of the poetic quest. This noise, perhaps like some life force, explodes in this section's final stanza as a prelude to Queneau's elaboration of the solar myth that he offers to account for his own paralysis: "Le coeur: sur le coeur je n'ai rien à dire / du silence à jamais détruit

/ le sourd balaye les débris / Le soleil: ô monstre, ô Gorgone, ô Méduse / ô soleil" (The heart: about the heart I have nothing to say / Silence forever destroyed / The deaf man sweeps away the debris / The sun: O monster, o Gorgon, o Medusa / o sun, 65). Queneau's emblematic gesture of sweeping, of purgation, leads to the discovery that the sun is to be equated with the Medusa, the Gorgon whose very look can petrify.

This identification is startling, to say the least, since Western culture has traditionally identified *helos*, the sun, with reason, with the father, with *logos* and the power to know. One might argue here that Queneau is seeking to reinterpret traditional solar mythology in order to subvert the psychoanalytic discourse that is also founded on this mythology. For insofar as psychoanalysis defends a principle of reason that is grounded in patriarchal ethics, insofar as the father's voice is identified with the individual and cultural superego, psychoanalysis is tributary of the solar myths that associate reason, *logos*, father, and light. Queneau is setting about to propose a different solar myth, one that undoes patriarchal supremacy even as it makes of the mother the source of his psychic impotence.

Recent scholarship has, moreover, turned up an essay that Queneau was working on in the early thirties, "Le symbolisme du soleil" (The symbolism of the sun). In this essay Queneau wished to demonstrate that a reading of primordial solar symbolism, especially with regard to the Minotaur and to the Gorgons, shows that the sun is identified with excrement and woman. We have already seen that Queneau calls the unfaithful "maternal sun" a "black excrement." In his essay Queneau went on to demonstrate that the primitive identification of the sun and excrement is also found in the language children use to describe the sun as well as in current French slang. The myth thus perdures in contemporary perceptions and children's mental structures. Whatever be the anthropological value of Queneau's essay (it is noteworthy that he did not publish it), it does throw some light on *Chêne et chien*, since Queneau incorporated parts of it directly into the second part's fourth section in which he attempts to revise psychoanalysis.

This section begins, however, with a notion taken from the literary crank Paul Roux's *Traité de la science de Dieu* (Treatise on the science of god). In his researches on literary madmen Queneau encountered in this writer the idea that the sun is the devil (70). This astounding proclamation, a résumé of Roux's theology, is followed by the equally surprising lines that identify the sun with a garbage can, a junkyard, a charnel house, and hell. Queneau offers a series of near-quotes from Roux's work to the effect that Satan took on the dress of the angel of light in order to deceive souls. Satan's inner kernel is excrement, where, notably, live the damned. Conjoined with this somewhat demented theological vision follow Queneau's several examples of how the sun can be identified with offal. The sun has been likened to an egg—hence a product of defecation—which is also shown by solstice rituals at Barcelonnette during which an omelette was offered to the sun. Emigration for Mexico frequently used to leave from this town, a fact that leads then by association to the evocation of the Indian priests of Uitzilopotchli who used to smear the sun's statue with *merde*. The sun resembles a gold louis coin, ergo, feces (Queneau took this example, as his essay shows, from one of Piaget's studies of children and language). The Minotaur, a sun god figure, is imprisoned in the labyrinth that Queneau, following Freud according to the earlier essay, interprets as an intestine. The Greek solar image of the triskelion, or three joined legs, figures an anus. And this image presents, according to the poem, the source of the poet's life. The source of his life is feminine putrefaction, since his life stems from the solar image as woman, the Gorgon or Medusa, the figure whose excremental tongue paralyzes him.

In this quite compressed development Queneau has effected a kind of double move. He has urged a psychoanalytic reading of culture and his own "castration" to undo psychoanalysis, primarily by recovering what he takes to be a more primitive myth underlying solar symbolism. He has also attempted to destroy the castrating father by turning him into a woman, into the Medusa whose severed head has turned the poet into the statue that cannot move. It seems plausible that Queneau's attraction to the identification of the sun and excrement is another manifestation of his penchant to experience all in terms of fall and decadence. But Queneau's solar myth is also an attempt to create a personal and poetic mythology that can grant him the personal autonomy to work in the real world. And this task is accomplished by creating a countermyth to our culture's reigning solar myth that, in its affirmation of the patriarchal and phallic values upon which psychoanalysis is founded, seemed to have nearly destroyed Queneau.

Queneau refuses to sustain this intensity, however, and the second part's fifth and sixth sections mark a return to the quotidian, to the most banal daily reality where neighbors play radios at night and one must walk across Paris in order to see one's psychoanalyst. Queneau mocks his doctor, yet continues to see him, for he is fascinated by this developing "detective story" in which the child is both criminal and victim: "for if deprived of love, you wanted to kill, child / you were the victim" (76).

The second part's seventh section offers another nautical metaphor, this one as an image of the poet's helplessness, for he sees himself as a shipwrecked vessel. The density of the development renders the passage somewhat obscure, but it seems that the poet likens himself and his naissant self ("this 'I' that makes a debut") to a boat that is about to sink to the depths of the sea. The comparison of the conscious mind to a ship afloat on the seas of the unconscious has become, at least since Rimbaud, a frequent image in modern poetry, and one can also see a surrealist influence in this choice of imagery. But Queneau is undertaking to revise our modernist notions about the poetic task; in this section the crew of the ship takes restorative measures, and the ship does *not* go under. The poet does not plunge into the darkness of the sea, perhaps into the depths of madness to find poetry. Rather, the ship moves into new waters where the buoys have not been destroyed and where, in the presence of these markings, the boat can move on toward new shores: "Voici: ce ne sont plus vers de faux rivages / que nous appareillons. / La vie est un songe, dit-on / mais deux c'est trop pour mon âge" (There it is: it is no longer toward false shores / that we are setting sail. / Life is a dream, they say, / but two is too many for my age, 78). Using the title of Calderon's seventeenth-century play to make mocking reference to psychoanalysis's belief that dream is the key to real psychic life, Queneau signifies his refusal to plunge into the abyss. No "Drunken Boat" like that described by Rimbaud, Queneau's vessel wants to set sail on the route of consciousness and lucidity.

The second part of *Chêne et chien* sets forth Queneau's other personal mythology, one that is inscribed in various ways throughout his poetry and novels. Queneau sees his persona figured by the oak and the dog. As Noel Arnaud has pointed out, Queneau was drawn to this rather strange juxtaposition by seeing in his own name the words *quêne,* or the Normand dialect form for "oak," and *quenêt* or *quenot,* dialect terms for "dog."[6] Queneau's reading of his name seems to be a way of using the Freudian interpretative grid of condensation that allows reading two antithetical meanings in one signifier, such as Freud frequently found in dream symbols. For Queneau, the oak and the dog represent opposing impulses, and thus his own name contains within it the contrasting forces of his own Manichean vision of gods and demons. The dog is the cynical beast (though sometimes an innocent victim, like the child uncovered by analysis); whereas the oak is the noble being that seeks in its immobile ascendancy to triumph over bestiality. With these symbols in hand, Queneau can reinterpret the biblical myth of the fall as an aspect of his personal mythology. The beast or the snake in paradise corrupted the tree of knowledge to bring about the loss of innocence—and leave Queneau hanging from the tree. In a very real sense, most of Queneau's life was, after the invention of this mythology, devoted to restoring innocence to knowledge. It was devoted to finding "the Sunday of life" during which knowledge could be undertaken as pure play, divested of all vestiges of the fall. One way of overcoming the fall is to find another vision of existence, such as in Oriental mythology: Queneau calls upon the Chinese "dragon to flame forth," to bring forth the hope that Christianity says we lost in the moment of original sin (82), and which psychoanalysis tells us we lose when we become adults.

Exorcising Cerberus, the three-headed dog that guards the entrance to Hades, Queneau can claim that he has seen "the shadows and phantoms" of the unconscious and that, with this recognition, "the filthy *(immonde)* . . . has disappeared" (83). At this point the reader may well feel that Queneau, in sublimating the "alchemical, black repressed," has completed a successful analysis even as he refuses the psychoanalytic reduction of psychic life to unconscious impulses. In *Chêne et chien,* Queneau does not, however, propose that there is such a thing as a psychoanalytic cure operating like some form of redemption. A quite different kind of redemption occurs in the poem. At the end of the second part the poet-oak rises up, loses his immobility, and begins the march toward the mountain where the fête takes place that concludes the poem. Triumph over the unconscious is a process of ascendancy to the mountain where the individual self breaks through its narcissistic limits in the collective overflowing of festival joy. Rabelais replaces Freud as a guide to redemption through the festive impulse.

In the poem's third part, called "La fête au village" ("The Village Festival"), the narrating "I" disappears. In this affirmation of the collective triumph of exuberance the isolated self, with its neuroses and complicity in guilt, has no place:

> Elle était si grande si grande la joie de leur coeur
> de joie
> qu'au-dessus des montagnes il dansait le soleil et
> qu'elle palpitait la terre
> qui porte les moissons
> Elle était si grande si grande la joie qu'elle
> jaillissait la rivière
> elle jaillissait la source entre les rochers et pissait
> en riant

> It was so great so great the joy of their heart of joy
> that above the mountains the sun danced and the earth
> throbbed
> the earth that bears crops
> Joy was so great so great that the river sprayed forth
> the spring sprayed forth between the rocks and pissed
> while laughing

(87)

Sterility is overcome in the festival uniting the collective body and the body of the earth in physical joy. Queneau's popular syntax creates a remarkable rhythm as it works to overcome all effects of separation by a kind of syntactic ambiguity in which joy, earth, and river seem interchangeable, and normally intransitive verbs acquire accusative accents. The reader must enter into the third part in festive participation, leaving the wasteland behind, in laughter and inebriation.

The fête and the festive impulse are dominant motifs throughout Queneau's work. They had already found implicit expression in Queneau's play with language and narrative forms in his first novel, *The Bark Tree* (1933). But one can say that the explicit affirmation of festival breaks forth at the end of *Chêne et chien*. This affirmation marks a central tendency in Queneau's poetic practice: Queneau increasingly moved away from the exploitation of a surrealist rhetoric in the service of melancholy as he wrote poems in which predominate a festive play with language and often popular motifs. This is not an absolute tendency, and Queneau's final work of poetry, *Morale élémentaire*, is in part as dark a work as any he wrote. The festival impulse must be understood as an ongoing process that offers its affirmation only in its enactment. In Queneau's case this enactment is often a festive transmutation of anguish and despair, a redemption achieved through comic play that is accompanied by a disabused recognition that the earthly paradise must be created anew at every moment.

Queneau's development of festive forms and his evolution away from his angry revolt against the fall seem to reflect the principle of selection for the choices, taken from three decades of work, that he published in his first collections of shorter poems: *Les Ziaux* in 1943, *L'Instant fatal* in 1946, and *Bucoliques* in 1947. Publishing *Les Ziaux* during the Nazi occupation of France, Queneau may have had little inclination for proposing other than somber reflections on destiny at this moment. *Les Ziaux* especially represents Queneau's saturnine temperament, with its recurrent nocturnal vision. The dominant tonality in this collection is melancholy, alternating between ironic lamentation and restrained anguish. The book offers poems that repeatedly use night as the decor in which man glimpses his ultimate truths: his separation from nature and his destiny as a being endowed with a consciousness of his own nothingness.

On a radio broadcast of his poems Queneau himself selected "Sourde est la nuit l'ombre la brume . . ." ("Deaf is night shadow fog . . .") to illustrate this knowledge that night brings.[7] In this poem's dignified anaphora Queneau repeats, as the first word for each line in each stanza, a word that stresses man's isolation in a silent world. *Deaf, blind, dumb,* and finally *infirm* are the repeated words that bind man and nature in a vision of their common fall: "Infirme est toute la nature / Infirmes sont bêtes et rocs / Infirme est la caricature / Infirme l'idiot qui débloque" (Infirm is all of nature / Infirm are beasts and rocks / Infirm is the caricature / Infirm is the idiot who blathers on, 65). This Shakespearean litany, with what probably should be taken as ironic self-reference in the last two lines, ends with an existential questioning that desires, uselessly, to go beyond the deaf, blind, and mute night: "Mais qui voit? qui entend? qui parle?" (But who sees? who hears? who speaks?, 65). The only answer would be the poet himself, man, the bizarre and forlorn creature who brings seeing, hearing, and speaking into the silent reign of infirmity.

Perhaps the most poignant nocturnal poem of the twenties is "Nuit" (Night), which Queneau published later in *L'Instant fatal*. This early poem shows an early influence of Chinese poetry on Queneau's cosmological lyricism. He begins the poem with a simple juxtaposition: "Nuit: une syllabe" (Night: a syllable, 114). Queneau first proposes, as it were, a definition of his poetic material that stands isolated on the page like juxtaposed characters. Next follows a descriptive juxtaposition in which walls are described as "closed like hexagons." The association of word and geometric figures, of night and walls, suggests a sense of enclosure that probably reflects a linguistic Platonism analogous to the mathematical Platonism Queneau held at the time: language and mathematics in their very materiality give access to the ultimately real world of forms and to the cosmos. Queneau seems here to entertain the idea that the definition of words might bring them into existence; hence an expanded definition of night, drawing upon Chinese cosmology and its association of night with the serpent: "Nuit: serpent troué d'anneaux rayon de l'arc-en-ciel" (Night: snake pierced with rings beam of the rainbow, 114). But with an exaggerated alliteration, Queneau adds a humorous twist that shows his own critical distance toward his cosmological impulse: the gods make dance the arches of letters forgotten among "moult mols muets mots" (many soft silent words). Dancing words, the cosmological serpent, a syllable—all this takes place within the confines of night in which being radiates and the world comes to be as it passes away. It is, however, the primordial power of nothingness that has the final word: "Tout semble s'évanouir même les montagnes agiles / Nuit" (All seems to fade even the nimble mountains / Night, 114).

Within the silence of Queneau's night, time appears as circular and cyclical. Time, as described in the early poems, is the process of the revelation of recurrent truths to an observer stripped of all pretension:

> Des jours se sont passés accompagnés de nuits
> des jours se sont passés longs de tout un parcours
> circulaire longs d'un grand soupir de soleil
>
> Days passed accompanied by nights
> days passed long with a great circular
> trajectory long with a great sigh of sun

(68)

Queneau's intuition of time as the circular repetition of the same processes undoubtedly underlies the attraction that repetitive poetic forms hold for him. Many of these and later poems are based on anaphora, litany, and other forms of rhythmic repetition. In a poem such as "Calme est l'arbre qui se dresse droit ou bien torve . . ." (Calm is the tree that arises straight or else askance . . .), the repetition of "calm" at the beginning of each of the seven lines produces an incantatory effect. This anaphora underscores the poet's determination to look upon the world with dignified resolve and to accept the "fixed course" that carries him away from Time (66). Or, in another poem of darkness, "Ombre descendue . . ." (Shadow descended . . .), the anaphora uses eighteen repetitions in a vision of the flight of all existence that concludes: "ombre est tout être qui s'enfuit" (Shadow is every being that flees, 72). Nothing perdures except the cosmic rhythms marking the disappearance of all that comes to be.

There is as much Baudelaire here as Heraclitus, the Greek philosopher who first gave us a metaphor that likens time to a river. Like Baudelaire, and like his favored Gnostic heretics, Queneau conceives time to be *le mal,* evil and anguish in all its senses. Queneau has, again, like Baudelaire, his poem on clocks, "L'Horloge," whose "little wheel isolates itself and never stops singing / it separates two seated men who shed tears . . ." (35). These two men are, as Queneau parenthetically says, himself and himself, which we might take to be the poet divided against himself, perceiving himself with Baudelairean lucidity as a witness of his forced obedience to the laws of time.

Queneau's trademark is, however, to have retained a whimsical sense of the daily fall into time that characterizes the most ordinary and trivial reality. With a comic nod to Verlaine, for example, he can note: "La mouche est morte au clair de lune" (A fly is dead in the moon light, 20). So much for octosyllabic lyricism; lyricism is, in Queneau's perspective, a minor aspect of poetry. For Queneau, in his poems and his novels, the test of literature would often be its capacity to account for the banal; and the tendency of all things to come apart and degrade is as much shown by the pigeon droppings covering Paris as by the philosopher or poet's anguish. Paris is the privileged place for finding the details of the fall; and it is not surprising that Queneau, in homage again to Baudelaire and Apollinaire, should have his poem on the city, "Amphion"; this Amphion does not, however, build cities: "Le Paris que vous aimâtes / n'est pas celui que nous aimons / et nous nous dirigeons sans hâte / vers celui que nous oublierons" (The Paris that you loved / is not the one that we love / and we go without haste / toward the one that we shall forget, 23). Cities and especially Paris are, for Queneau, the scene of a kind of double nothingness in which one heads toward a forgetting of what has already disappeared: only old maps provisionally remain to recall that buildings, sites, streets, all were once different and will be different soon again.

Self-referentiality is a feature of Queneau's work that has many functions throughout his poetry and novels. In "L'Explication des métaphores," one of the most powerful poems of *Les Ziaux* and one that has become an anthology piece, self-referentiality acts as a kind of existential self-questioning. As the title suggests, this "explication of metaphors" asks what meaning, if any, can be wrested from the universe by arbitrary poetic structures. In the first stanza Queneau gives us a portrait of man, reduced to his essential traits, that recalls the kind of reduction one might find in a Giacometti sculpture work: man is thrown out of time and space, "thin as a hair, ample as the dawn," with his nostrils frothing and his eyes rolled back as he attempts to feel some decor about himself—a decor that the second stanza declares to be nonexistent. This reduction of man to a cosmic searcher carries with it the question about the sense of such a reduction. What, the poem asks, can be the sense of such "metaphors" that make of man a hair or the dawn.

No answer is available. The poet can only enunciate the paradoxes, like those of the Taoist thinkers or of his favored pre-Socratic Parmenides, that are involved in any attempt to name what is: "Si je parle du temps, c'est qu'il n'est pas encore, / Si je parle d'un lieu, c'est qu'il a disparu, / Si je parle d'un homme, il sera bientôt mort, / Si je parle du temps, c'est qu'il n'est déjà plus . . ." (If I speak of time, it does not exist yet, / If I speak of a place, it has disappeared, / If I speak of a man, he will soon be dead, / If I speak of time, it no longer is . . . , 75). He can say that there are gods, but these gods resemble man in every respect; and one can only ask the same question about the meaning of the metaphor that describes them. These gods might well appear to be the forces in man that push him to "hatch iron" or to "gather coal" or to "distill cinnabar"— the latter being a reputedly magic compound in popular Taoism. In short, the gods are restless demons, generated dialectically as

"reflections, negative images" of the more primordial immobility
and nothingness (76).

But man is neither god nor demon, and at the poem's conclusion
the poet can only reiterate his description of man, who finally is
not "thin nor ample" enough. He is the sum of his tortured muscles
and his used up spittle, with only one hope: "Le calme reviendra
lorsqu'il verra le Temple / De sa forme assurer sa propre éternité"
(Calm will return when he sees the Temple / Of his form fix his
own eternity, 77). Tortured physically and metaphysically, man
must transform his own image as a carnal being. This transformation
is the work of creation that the poem proposes. As Wladimir Krysinski puts it in an essay on "L'Explication des métaphores," man
must himself be the creator of form, the bearer and inventor of
metaphors.[8] To which one might add that this creation is demanded
even when it can have no ultimate sense, when there is no "explication of metaphors."

Published in 1946 L'Instant fatal is something of a companion
volume to Les Ziaux, since this collection again offers a selection of
poems taken from the same three decades of writing. Queneau takes
care to date the first section of the collection, "Marine," to show
that these poems are all from the twenties, and two other sections
are dated to show that the poems were written primarily during
and immediately after the Occupation. Later editions have an ad-
ditional section, "Pour un art poétique," that includes poems about
poetry that were also published in Bucoliques in 1947. This division
corresponds to a difference of tonality in the different groups of
poems. The poems written by the very young Queneau in "Marine"
are in large part more of his melancholy surrealist work. In the
current edition's second section, "Un enfant a dit," Queneau has
grouped poems in which the dominant mood is generated by a
child's vision, especially a child's joy in language play; whereas in
the fourth section of this edition, "L'Instant fatal"—the fatal moment—are found slangy, often parodistic works of black comic
intent that many take to be most typical of Queneau. Queneau's
love of comic incongruity is also evident in his unorthodox descriptions of his "poetic art."

The works in "Marine" using surrealist rhetoric, or systematically
irrational juxtapositions, confront the reader with the greatest problems of comprehension, for these texts often give the impression of
being allegories for which no conceptual key is available. One is

tempted to read them in terms of Queneau's recurrent imagery, for recurrence seems to promise a minimal meaning. The first poem of "Marine," also called "Marine" ("Seascape"), teasingly asks the reader to make sense of its medusae and sharks: "Les poissons ont de si jolies têtes / qu'on est obligé de les déplacer fréquemment / à cause des ravages qu'ils font dans le coeur des méduses" (Fish have such pretty heads / that one is obliged to move them frequently / because of the havoc they play with the medusae's hearts, 87). Queneau's probable equivocation of Medusas and jellyfish (or medusae) suggests that the petrifying goddesses of his personal mythology can appear as the aquatic life that terrifies him in its otherness. On the other hand, the poem's sharks, making "pretty sheets for the clever ones who have drowned," suggest little more than a rather acerbic appreciation, full of the black humor that Queneau later rejected, of the comforts of nature. Biographical readings often yield little for these poems.

Other surrealist texts in *L'Instant fatal* are, however, nearly programmatic quests for the marvelous that André Breton had declared to be the goal of all surrealist activity. Part of this quest in poetry entails a rather systematic dislocation of normal semantic relationships. In "L'aube évapore le nouveau-né" (Dawn evaporates the newborn child) one finds that "Le calme désert allume le calumet de la paix" (The calm desert lights up the peace pipe, 148). This line typically respects normal grammar, syntax, and even some semantic motivation: the desert uses the pipe for its normal function, smoking, and does not, say, eat the pipe. The marvelous resides, one supposes, in the incongruous description of an activity that normal "logic" would not find possible, and which seemingly has no figural meaning. There is something rather mechanical in the way this surrealist writing, respecting most linguistic codes, singles out irrational semantic juxtapositions that do occasionally offer a sense of discovery. Of course, this mechanical slide may well have appealed to the future cofounder of Oulipo.

More interesting in Queneau's surrealist texts is the self-referential dimension by which they designate themselves as quests for the marvelous. Perhaps most surrealist poems have this metalinguistic aspect; it is in any case the single most fruitful approach, I believe, for generating meaning in Queneau's surrealist work. In the same poem in which dawn disposes of the new baby, Queneau describes the quest for poetic analogy by saying that "The words that did

without the shadows of reality / Died . . ." (119). This description
of language, embedded in the context of the poem itself, must
designate the poem's own attempt to grasp "the shadows of reality,"
or the surreality that would be the poem's ultimate goal. Words
that die, that fall perhaps from the poetic state of grace, must become
in this poem workers or boxers in order to earn a living. A figural
reading suggests that, for the surrealist Queneau as for Mallarmé,
fallen language enters the marketplace, or the sports arena, from
which the poetic marvelous is excluded. Queneau appears at this
point to be subscribing to the modernist myth of two languages,
one Orphic and poetic, the other destined to use and destruction.
Reading Queneau's surrealist poems as allegories about their own
language does not "explain" every element in them, but it does
allow one to see that even for the young Queneau one task of poetry
was to explore its own nature; and part of that exploration surely
involved the Orphic quest that aimed at triumphing over the fallen
nature of language—as well as the rest of creation in Queneau's
view.

Queneau's work also has a referential dimension. Poems in *L'Instant fatal,* as well as a good many in *Les Ziaux* and *Bucoliques,* refer
sufficiently often to Queneau's experience of war so as to make one
believe that the prospect of another war, and then the experience
of the Occupation, were a watershed experience that tempered Queneau's revolt. The destruction brought about by war and the oppres-
sion suffered under the Nazis rendered derisive any revolt grounded
in a petulant distaste for bourgeois society. More philosophically,
war, as experienced indirectly by the child and then directly by the
adult, may have confirmed how fallen man is, but with such atro-
cious proofs that only tragic acceptance could keep someone like
Queneau from going mad. Queneau was no longer a rebel after the
Occupation, and the grounds for this change are to be found in
many poems written before that time.

The carnality of death and the *déchéance* of flesh are made manifest,
for example, in the terse lines found in "La Guerre" (War), written
in 1927 and published in *Bucoliques:* "comme la semence déposée
au hasard des routes / cadavres vermolus à peine éphémères" (like
seed thrown blindly along roads / worm-eaten cadavers barely transitory, 21). This vision of war, drawn from the mass slaughter of
World War I, finds in *L'Instant fatal* a more abstract counterpart
in another poem written in the twenties, "Les Thermopyles" (The

thermopylae), a title referring to the narrow pass where the Spartans fought against the Persians in 480 B. C. Queneau's purpose in this latter poem is not to write a historical poem about the glorious massacre in which the Greeks sacrificed themselves. Rather this poem offers a generalized meditation upon the recurring disasters of human experience for which this battle—and perhaps any battle—can be emblematic. Queneau views all human experience as a form of repetition, and in a sense any battle is a recurrence of what happened in the Thermopylae. Here essential experience is metonymically rendered in the cries of the dying: "plusieurs n'ont pas vécu plus que le soupir / du destin enclavé dans la perle des dents / du désastre accroupi sous les arceaux ardents / arceaux ardant le corps du blessé qui gémit" (some lived no longer than the sigh / of destiny enclosed within the teeth's pearl / of disaster crouched under burning arches / arches burning the body of the wounded one who moans, 93). Queneau's attitude toward war and the destiny it embodies is expressed here in a modernist attempt to extract essential structures—forms of essential revelation, if one prefers—from specific historical experience to which the poem implicitly refers. Queneau often attempts to transcend historical particularity and, as a result, his work often appears to deny historical specificity.

This approach to experience can create interpretative problems. For example, Queneau did not date "Isis," published in *Les Ziaux* during the Occupation; and without a specific historical context the poem has a hyperbolic tonality that nothing within the poem quite seems to justify: "Ces longs ponts traversant les cieux brillent de gloire / et sacrifient leur arche aux multiples couleurs / le vert gémit parfois le bleu dans sa douleur / saigne comme un vrai dieux auquel il nous faut croire" (These long bridges crossing the heavens shine with glory / and sacrifice their arch with multiple colors / green moans at times blue in its pain / bleeds like a real god in which we must believe, 28). The reader familiar with French poetry will note a kind of reply to Apollinaire's line, in "La Chanson du malaimé" (The song of the badly loved), calling unhappiness a god in which we must not believe. Yet, it is not altogether clear what is the pain that motivates the presence of unhappiness, unless it be another general expression of Queneau's saturnine temperament. Claude Debon, however, has shown that the poem was written in 1940 during the exodus before the German invasion forces, when civilization itself seems to have collapsed.[9] Within this context the poem's claim that the "Theater of the World" is "illustrated by horror" has more than plausibility, and the reader can assent to the poem's proposition that Isis, messenger of the gods and goddess of the rainbow, is also a messenger of catastrophe even as the rainbow shines mockingly in glory. It is only with this double perspective, offered by the modernist quest for the essential word and the specific historical reference, that the reader can find a coherent reading for the second stanza's image of the night that "lets sink without sails / the uncertain galleon of anguish and tears." Night is the time of dissolution in Queneau, and in "Isis" we find a modernist elegy on the way nature both participates in and is indifferent to our disasters, nature that, as "echoes without will," offers "very faithful mirrors" of our destruction.

To be read in counterpoint to "Isis," with its oblique reference to a history it would deny, is "Le Havre de Grâce," published in *L'Instant fatal*. This later poem shows Queneau's greater willingness to respect historical specificity and might be viewed as a sign of his movement away from the modernist attempt to translate all experience into abstract revelation. The title gives an ambivalent context, but a context nonetheless, for it may be read either as Le Havre, Queneau's place of birth, or as "the haven of grace," perhaps with reference to childhood memories. Published immediately after the war, the poem portrays Queneau's reaction to the destruction that Le Havre had undergone from aerial bombardments. Reduced to an "obscure scrap-heap" the city offered no place in which to look for "time or memory" (192). The city, in its presence, offers nothing: "Les plans retraceront cette topographie / Les archives créeront cette chronologie / La mort s'affirme pure au creux des brèches sèches" (Maps will trace again this topography / Archives will create this chronology / Death is affirmed in a pure state in the hollow of the dry breaches, 192). Man may give himself the illusion of lasting in time by creating maps and archives, by creating a fictive past in the future, but the poet sees that death and destruction mock these illusions here. Seeing that "memories are already beginning to die," Queneau's poet can have recourse to only one gesture: to seek a broom with which to sweep away the waste: "Un balai un balai pour toute la poussière / Je suis si mort déjà que je puis rire aux larmes / Et la mer lessivait ce qui veut bien blanchir" (A broom a broom for all the dust / I'm already so dead that I can laugh till I cry / And the sea laundered out whatever would wash, 193). This is the image of man's task throughout Queneau's work: to collaborate, in his modest way, with the purification of the dissolution that wreaks havoc throughout the cosmos. Sweeping is Queneau's humble gesture of cosmic acceptance.

"Le Havre de Grâce" ends on the image of laughter wrung from defeat. Pointing to the Nietzschean laughter that concludes *Pierrot,* this image also brings us back to the festive impulse that we saw concluding *Chêne et chien.* Especially in *L'Instant fatal* and *Bucoliques* does Queneau develop often comic forms of festive play with language. These forms of play usually entail borrowings from popular French and billingsgate, though Queneau is also a great inventor of neologisms, puns, and deformations. In one sense this is an aspect of his neoclassicism, for he often does quite literally what the seventeenth-century reformer poet Malherbe prescribed: he goes to the workers to find the language of his poems. Or, to go back to the Renaissance for a comparison, one can say that Queneau does not hesitate to use the language of the marketplace, that great source of festive and parodistic language that the Russian critic Bakhtin found to be the major source of Rabelais's parodistic verve. The play with language, bringing in the most earthy language of the marketplace, represents in Queneau's work a kind of parodistic critique of the pretensions of modernism. Which is to say that Queneau's range as a poet is quite extraordinary: he is capable of using the festive aggression of popular language to counter his own impulses to seek the essential language of modernist poetic revelation.

The poems grouped in "L'Instant fatal," the fourth section of the collection of this name, offer the best introduction to Queneau's poems that, combining slang and traditional forms, work in their violation of traditional poetic norms to renew the commonplaces of lyric poetry. Festive aggression is ultimately not destructive, though its systematic transgression may well reduce the pretensions of sanctified cultural forms. Consider in this respect how Queneau treats Ronsard's version of the traditional carpe diem motif. In a poem that every schoolchild in France knows, "Mignonne, allons voir si la rose . . ." Ronsard compares a rose and a young girl to prove that the girl should "seize the day." (Herrick's "To the Virgins, to Make Much of Time" is an English version of the same motif.) In his "Si tu t'imagines," a poem that became a hit song, Queneau uses popular Parisian slang to make the same point and goes on to elaborate in terms of grotesque realism how much the girl "will

blow it" if she does not make the most of the moment: "très sournois
s'approchent / la ride véloce / la pesante graisse / le menton triplé
/ le muscle avachi . . ." (very slyly approaches / the rapid wrinkle
/ the heavy fat / the triple chin / falling-down muscles . . . , 182).
In this poem, as in other pseudoballads and mock litanies, Queneau
introduces the bodily grotesque as a way of affirming the primacy
of the language of carnal reality as well as the disabused laughter
of the popular wisdom that this language embodies.

As Jacques Guicharnaud has observed about Queneau's work in
general, most of the poems in "L'Instant fatal" are not parodistic
of specific works, though nearly all are parodistic distortions of the
received topoi of high culture concerning love, growing old, and
dying.[10] Queneau's poems give voice to the festive impulses that
counter destructive physiological processes by frank recognition of
their inevitable nature. The "fatal moment" is a cliché, but when
it is celebrated in mock distichs, using classical metric forms, written in the language of the marketplace, death becomes a kind of
medieval morality character that one can encounter with mocking
lucidity:

> Quand nous pénétrerons la gueule ed' de travers
>       dans l'empire des morts
> avecque nos verrues nos poux et nos cancers
>       comme en ont tous les morts
>
> When we enter with our kisser turned around
>       the kingdom of the dead
> withe our tumors our lice and our cancers
>       like all the dead have
>
>                                      (167)

Forty-one stanzas of this litany, so many cyclic recurrences of the
body's collapse on the way to death, serve to valorize one final
platitude: "the fatal moment will always come to distract us" (170).
The very length of the litany, with its irony created by a self-
conscious use of popular language, renews even as it demonstrates
the futile wisdom that the cliché embodies.

The poem's self-conscious irony also turns on the poet's awareness
of himself as a mere cell in the great body of human development.
He is merely one comic exemplar of the recurrent cycles of physiological laws: "J'ai pris le pucelage / de la maturité / Me voilà qui

grisonne / me voilà qui bedonne / je tousse et je déconne . . ."
(I've taken on the virginity / of maturity / Here I am growing gray
/ taking on a paunch / I cough and speak bloody rubbish . . . ,
171). Stressed by the comic rhymes, the poet's stance toward himself
in "Vieillir" (Growing old) is a self-reflexive deprecation of his own
effort to do anything other than parody himself.

Growing old is but one step in humanity's fall leading to the
grave. Childhood precedes, and Queneau underscores his desire to
re-create the vision of a certain childhood by calling the second
section of *L'Instant fatal* "Un enfant a dit" (A child said). Many of
Queneau's poems written in the forties, in *L'Instant fatal* and *Bucoliques,* are texts in which he seems to delight in the primordial
presence of words as physical things, much as a child takes joy in
playing with words as sounds, delighting in their combinative possibilities and the infinite permutations they allow. Queneau's delight
in words for their own sake would seem to be another aspect of his
strategy for recovering innocence in that fallen world in which the
child Queneau found guilt to be universal. In this respect Queneau's
festive play with language might be likened to existentialist attempts
to proclaim what Albert Camus saw as man's essential innocence.
By playing with language even anguish can be stripped of its mor-
bidity. In "Affreux mur" (Awful wall) the poet transforms his
existential questioning into a linguistic game: "où-suis-jur? / où
suis-joye? / où suis-juis?"—all variants on "Where am I?" (139).
And if the answer is nowhere, the poet also admits that it is all "un
jeu simple / que j'invimple / dans la nuimple" (a simple game /
that I inventle / in the nightle, 139).

Inventing games in the night is a good description of much of
Queneau's later poetry. In "Bois II" (Woods II) of *Bucoliques* the
poet, playing like a child with the combinative possibilities of
phonemes, creates a forest that has surrealistic overtones: "Sapins /
Pins sapins pins pins / Abrichênes arbricauts / Arbres de cristaux"
(67). The sounds of "firs" and "pines" in French offer rhymes that
then motivate new rhyming combinations, giving a "tree-oak" and
a "tree-cot," suggesting an apricot; and the entire game finds a
résumé with "crystal trees," trees created from the crystalline mol-
ecules of combining phonemes. No reader of Joyce would have much
trouble with this kind of play, nor with the multiple kinds of puns,
nonsense play, double entendre, as well as the straight parody that
runs throughout Queneau's poetry. The earlier collection *Les Ziaux*

also includes some of this play. The title of this collection and of the concluding poem, for example, is a neologism that combines "waters" and "eyes"—*eaux* and *yeux*—in a single word expressing a kind of baroque conceit about their unity in a single mutually reflecting gaze. Or one of Queneau's most successful self-referential puns in this collection is "muses et lézards"—muses and lizards, or, in French, "the arts." Finally, one of his most successful festive parodies, "Le repas ridicule" (The ridiculous meal), rewrites classical satires by Horace, Régnier, and Boileau by telling, with a contemporary Parisian accent, the tale of a meal that is, as in much of Queneau's culinary satire, frankly disgusting.

As the example of rewriting a classical satire shows, Queneau's play with literary forms is often a reflection on the conditions of possibility of literature itself and on how literary forms and genres are ways of organizing our experience of the world. As a final example of this type of literature about literature let us cite what is perhaps Queneau's best-known work, his *Exercises de style,* first published in 1947. This work escapes easy classification, since it is at once a "narrative," the same narrative repeated ninety-nine times, and has been produced as a play. It is certainly a work of poetry insofar as it shows that literature can freely exploit language in multiple ways. In these "exercises," like a musician exploring variations on a theme, Queneau takes one banal incident and uses ninety-nine different styles to narrate the same events. Style here means both possible arrangements of the events and choice of diction and vocabulary. The events are minimal: someone gets on a bus, his feet are stepped on, and he appears again at some later time in front of a train station where a friend seems to give him advice about a button on his coat.

The game consists in taking this anecdotal material, selecting a given "style" as a kind of constraint, and then inventing a text that forces the material to illustrate the style. If the stylistic constraint is to use understatement, then the text becomes a series of litotes: "Some of us were travelling together. A young man, who didn't look very intelligent, spoke to the man next to him for a few moments, then he went and sat down. Two hours later I met him again; he was with a friend and was talking about clothes."[11] It can be done in a "metaphorical" style:

In the centre of the day, tossed among the shoal of travelling sardines in a coleopter with a big white carapace, a chicken with a long, featherless neck suddenly harangued one, a peace-abiding one, of their number, and its parlance, moist with protest, was unfolded upon the airs. Then, attracted by a void, the fledgling precipitated itself thereunto.

In a bleak, urban desert, I saw it again that self-same day, drinking the cup of humiliation offered by a lowly button. (24)

The Japanese haiku, with the quantitative restriction of seventeen syllables, imposes even more demanding constraints:

> Summer S long neck
> plait hat toes abuse retreat
> station button friend
> (139)

And, with ninety-six other variants, including negativities, anagrams, onomatopoeia, logical analysis, and (in Barbara Wright's English translation) Cockney, Queneau demonstrates that "literarity"—the nature of literary language—is to work with, if not against, preconceived constraints that function as so many game-rules for the genesis of a text.

This decision to work with arbitrary constraints is in a sense neoclassicism, but with a vengeance. Queneau flaunts the indifference of the fable or material to be narrated. One might imagine that he had in mind the situation of the classical poet when a patron ordered a version of "Andromache" or "Iphigenia"—and perhaps the ninety-ninth version of the same. There is of course a notable difference between Queneau and a neoclassical poet such as Racine or Goethe, to name two poets who penned an "Iphigenia." For Queneau also flaunts the very triviality of his anecdote by highlighting that is drawn from the most quotidian reality. Noble subjects no longer seem to exist, Queneau implies; or, as we said at the outset of this chapter, there are no privileged subjects for art, and the contemporary writer must have recourse to life as it exists after the fall. The absurd and arbitrary story of bus-taking and foot-crushing (to use a participial style) can only be material, with ninety-nine repetitions, for the comedy of fallen existence. Queneau is the great comic poet of our daily banality.

## Chapter Three
# Cosmological Visions and Other Games: The Later Poetic Texts

In 1950 Queneau published one of the most extraordinary poems written in French—or in any other language—in the twentieth century: his *Petite cosmogonie portative.* His game plan for this long poem was to write in six cantos a modern cosmography that sets forth the origins of the world and of life therein. Queneau draws liberally upon the knowledge that scientific disciplines could provide in the forties, but his work is also an homage to the Latin poet Lucretius and his *On the Nature of Things,* a cosmological work in six cantos that is the *locus classicus* for an Epicurean and atomistic worldview in antiquity. Drawing upon modern physics, chemistry, geology, astronomy, and especially biology, Queneau clearly intends to expand the boundaries of poetic discourse. In his cosmography he mixes Parisian slang, neologisms, puns, and language taken from generally nonpoetic diction with a great variety of technical terms taken from scientific discourses. Modern science, with its accelerating growth of special terminologies, has greatly augmented the weight of our dictionaries; and Queneau's bet in writing this poem is that these new terminologies can become part of the game of modern poetic expression. As the writer and critic Max Bense puts it in his introduction to the German translation, Queneau speaks here about things, but only insofar as things are words.[1]

In typically self-reflexive fashion Queneau addresses within the poem itself the question of the poem's diction and its lexicon. He does not raise the question, however, until the third canto when, in describing the chemical elements in the periodic table, he comes to mercury, the only classical god among the elements. He then asks this deity, also known as Hermes, to explain the goal of this linguistic feast that, by this point, may have left many a reader a little perplexed. Hermes, messenger of the gods, announces a new poetic diction that, in *not* comparing young girls to rose petals, finds in each science a "boiling register": "Les mots se gonfleront du suc de toutes choses / de la sève savante et du docte latex" (Words will swell with the substance of all things / with the sap of knowledge and learned latex, 128).[2] Poets have traditionally drawn upon a limited lexicon, one made up of flowers, myths, and symbols. But Queneau will sing of pitchblende and electromagnetism, even if, in a strict sense, he does not know what they are—any more than do poets who sing of roses.

This skepticism about knowledge in the poem springs from Queneau's belief that we never know things in themselves, only relations between them. These relations can be given by words, presumably all words, for Queneau is calling for poetic equality for all the words in the dictionary, whether or not they were used by Racine, Hugo, or Mallarmé. Queneau is calling for a truly expanded notion of intertextual practice that will allow all texts, with all their words, to enter into the poem; in this case, all the various scientific texts that go to make up a total vision of what we take to be reality. And with this vocabulary he also includes all the festive language that comes from the marketplace.

Queneau's cosmography draws in part upon biology and geology to tell the story of evolution from the primal nebulae to the appearance of contemporary machine intelligence. One might expect this narration to lend itself to a linear development, beginning with the cosmic explosion that produced the earth, and then following the series of chemical accidents that allowed inanimate substances to combine and give rise to the subsequent evolutionary course that life has taken. Queneau skips about a great deal, however, and relies upon synopses to keep the reader informed as to where the poet is in the course of evolution. Part of Queneau's refusal of linear coordination is an aesthetic question: he wishes to represent the simultaneous development of all aspects of the earth and its evolution through a kind of collage that emulates the multiple processes at work in the universe. But Queneau is also most interested in the passage from inanimate to animate matter, and he returns to this question several times. One might say that his primary interest is to create a mythic image of the passage from the inorganic to the organic—of the cosmic leap that led to man and, through man, to machine intelligence.

In his review of the poem in 1951 the biologist Jean Rostand
said Queneau's view of evolution was essentially correct.[3] Today,
however, readers may have some trouble imagining why Queneau
was so fascinated by the role of the tobacco mosaic virus in the
evolution of life, for contemporary biologists generally assume that
viruses could only arise after the development of cells. On the basis
of research done by scientists in the thirties, Queneau seems to have
speculated that the virus was the link between inanimate and animate matter. Typical of this research was work done by Wendell
M. Stanley. He received the Nobel Prize for chemistry in 1946
because of his work in the thirties when he isolated a crystalline
protein having the infectious properties of the tobacco mosaic virus.
This crystalline substance seemed to have some of the properties
associated with living organisms, which allowed speculation that
this protein might be considered a chemical having vitalist properties. In other words a crystalline formation would be the link to
cellular development. Queneau certainly found this image attractive,
for he returns to it several times in his cosmography. Crystals becoming life is perhaps the central mythic image in the poem, reflecting a kind of vitalism that has little place in contemporary
evolutionary theory or cellular biology. But Queneau was writing
before the work of Crick and Watson.

Queneau has written a poem, however, not a work of biology,
and it is precisely its mythic value that interests us (and much of
it, of course, is still consonant with contemporary scientific models).
Queneau's effort to describe, in all its chaos, the earth's birth in
the first canto is as much indebted to the Greeks as to astrophysics,
for the very biological metaphor of birth points to an animistic view
of the cosmos and its processes. Images of the bodily grotesque
dominate in this parturition, and Queneau's image of the cosmic
body gives another expression to the festive impulse. As in Rabelais,
birth is a corporeal explosion: the "demented earth" "puckers up
like the ass of a dried up mummy" as it spews forth its exploding
"varicose veins" in its rejuvenation (98–99). Or, in another biological metaphor, the earth seems to merge as in cell mitosis where
the nucleus splits: "et fendu comme une fesse / altère une autre noix
où les fils filiformes / gênent de leurs néants les possibles qui dor-
ment" (and split like a buttock / changes another nut where filiform
threads / disturb with their nothingness the possible beings that are
asleep, 99). This genetic metaphor expresses the Leibnizian cast to

Queneau's cosmography, for evolution is the sorting out of possible beings that can come to existence out of the nothingness or nonbeing that contains them. These "possibles" seem to be contained, like Leibniz's monads within God's mind, within the idea of existence itself, perhaps as generated by the possibilities of mathematical combination that underwrites the genesis of forms. Such a view affirms a necessarily rational structure to the universe.

In this view a cosmography tells the unfolding of possibilities contained within the primal nebulae whose explosion gives birth to the earth and then to life. Within this nebulae are contained the numbers that preside over the organization of biological forms, and thus are capable of sexually engendering the world: numbers are "fish-hooks of zeroes" that were "cooking" in the primitive atom and now valiantly ride out the explosion of birth (102). Or, to continue the culinary metaphor, nothingness eats a lunch of "possibilities stewed into an identity." This Leibnizian cuisine cooks up a burlesque solar system in which Queneau parodies each of the planets for what its name might suggest, such as Venus a prostitute, or Mercury a businessman. But it is only on earth that the culinary possibilities exist for the "bouillon" to cook up the crystalline viruses that Queneau presents at the end of the first canto in a celebration of the emergence of life forms. Attracted undoubtedly by the geometric nature of crystals, our contemporary Lucretius sings of the copulating fecundity with which crystals participate in the birth of being, "planting in the avid matrixes of the ground / bringing about the exact term in vague ovaries" (106).

Queneau's bucolic vein vibrates in the second canto's paean to the appearance of plant life and, with this energy source, the emergence of animal life in the universe. The mystery of the passage from inanimate to living matter appears again as a kind of vitalist promise wherein "crystals mixed in mineral being / raised themselves fructifying toward that freedom / that a heavy molecular weight was promising" (114). This passage to freedom finds a partial explanation in Queneau's brief allusion to Mendel and the laws of genetics that the Austrian discovered (114), but Queneau is more interested here, as in the rest of the poem, in celebrating the mathematical forms underlying existence. "Father polyhedron" gives rise to living forms, overcoming entropy, and allowing the "hairless crystal" to realize its entelechy as an albuminous cell (and the use of Aristotle's term *entelechy* for life's goal shows Queneau's rationalist allegiance in this poem to a kind of teleological thought).

A tragic sense also accompanies this description of the proliferation of life forms, for many forms have appeared and have failed to perdure. Queneau has a tragic feeling for the individuals as well as for the species that have disappeared in the course of evolution. The second canto concludes with lines that are classical in simplicity and grandeur, recalling so many individuals that have attempted to impose their species and have been "swept away" by the earth (118). In this failure individuals die a double death, their own and their species—for the earth buries all (119).

Never hesitating to mix modern and antique, Queneau borrows from the pre-Socratic philosopher Empedocles the image of an ideal sphere to set forth a model of the periodic table of elements. He then proceeds to describe, with numerous plays on words and erudite allusions, the elements; but breaks off his description with the twenty-first element, scandium, claiming that he has no more space for the description if he is to do justice to his subject matter. However, one feels that Queneau is more fascinated by the adventures of biology than by the fixed classifications of chemistry. In the fourth canto he returns to the passage from the crystal to the virus and speculates that polarized light might have "asymmetrized" crystals and given birth to the tobacco mosaic virus. Queneau is skeptically amused by his own speculation, since he notes that this genealogy would allow one to claim that a sapphire is the ancestor of the common cold (137).

The fourth canto is an evocation of the lower orders of the animal kingdom, though man is not absent from these considerations. Man's eventual presence as the final product of the animal kingdom, as the implicit "goal" of all past animal reproduction, allows Queneau to include a long section on *volupté*—the sexual impulse—in a festive celebration of the evolution of sexual development. Parodying Lucretius's invocation of Venus at the outset of *On the Nature of Things*, Queneau calls nature our lovely "erectoress" *(banditrix)* that encouraged the first sexed being to shoot his sperm into his female double. For the festive mind the sexual impulse is never dark, but rather a source of parodistic and mirthful celebration. Queneau's sense of the comedy of eros is perhaps nowhere more succinctly expressed than when he muses that "Y a beaucoup à parier que l'unicellulaire / n'avait pas dû prévoir que le métazoaire / prendrait tant de plaisir à grimper sa moitié" (You can bet that unicellular beings didn't foresee that the metazoans / would take such pleasure in mounting on their better half, 140). The spirit of carnivalesque truth underwrites this comic view of evolution, making of it the science of unending copulation.

Queneau breaks off this development in the fifth canto to return to a description of the plant kingdom, although this development serves largely to sing praises of photosynthesis—which is to say the source of all animal existence. Returning to the animal kingdom to describe briefly insects, Queneau then develops a long section on cordates, the phylum of which man is a member. Queneau may deflate man at the beginning of the sixth canto by reducing his presence in the cosmos to two lines: "The monkey (or his cousin) the monkey became man / the one who a bit later split the atom" (162). But man's presence as the observer who constructs the model of evolution is superimposed throughout these cantos. Science itself is a product of evolution, and in a sense the possibility for science must be contained within that evolutionary past. Evolution exists only because man is a creator who in his "anatomical dream" can "incline this crowd of beasts / toward the network of classifications" (155). As ontogeny recapitulates phylogeny, so Queneau's cosmography contains within itself the story of its own genesis, of man's turning toward the evolutionary past and finding all of life inscribed within himself.

But man is not the stopping point of evolution, and the sixth and final canto recapitulates those inventions which, through human agency, have continued evolution in the form of history. As Queneau makes clear in his *Une Histoire modèle,* he views inventions as the only elements of change that can cause historical development in any meaningful sense. Machines begin with the simplest exploitation of natural forces—streams or fire—and develop, like life forms, into increasingly complex structures. In Queneau's perspective machines then begin to propagate themselves (169) and increasingly resemble living organisms. Queneau was writing at the time when the "Turing machine" first allowed us to speak of machine intelligence, though before the revolution in integrated circuitry put a computer in every home. But the possibilities for artificial intelligence that existed in the forties were sufficiently developed for Queneau to speculate on the increasing development of machine intelligence as the next stage in evolution. "Saurians of calculus" join "bipeds" in knowing how to count and talk, talk and count, since machines now take on mathematics and language for their uses. Queneau's cosmography comes to end with a series of repetitions that make one wonder, however, if the future belongs to stuck records or to prolix machines. In any case, the future belongs to language, even if spoken by an electronic voice.

Queneau's *Petite cosmogonie portative* is Joycean in its attempt to synthesize the festive impulse in language with a didactic desire to utilize the full resources of the lexicon, especially those resources the poet can find in modern science. After this homage to the observing biped—scientific man—Queneau's poetic work goes in a number of directions, though none of them demonstrates the lexical mania that makes his cosmography such a linguistic fête. Between 1958 and 1975 Queneau published six major collections of poetry and a seventh work, *Cent mille milliards de poèmes,* whose potential for giving the reader one hundred thousand billion sonnets seems to defy the simple designation as a "collection." In terms of their current availability, however, Queneau's later poetic works are a bit easier to keep track of. His *Le Chien à la mandoline* and his *Sonnets,* both published in 1958, are now available in a single, considerably augmented edition, published in 1965 as *Le Chien à la mandoline* (The dog with a mandolin). Three volumes, *Courir les rues, Battre la campagne,* and *Fendre les flots,* published in successive years from 1967 to 1969, have appeared in one volume as a single trilogy. The enigmatic *Morale élémentaire*—elementary morals or moral treatise—is edited in a single volume, as befits a book that Queneau supposedly should have liked to have published under a pseudonym. All his poetry will, in a not too distant future, be available in a single Pléiade volume.

In *Le Chien à la mandoline* the reader who has followed Queneau's poetic career encounters a reasonably familiar poetic universe. As the collection's title suggests, Queneau stages his poetic presence in an even more self-conscious manner in many of these poems. His dog-self is on stage, though with a musical instrument, a sign that this fallen beast of flesh aspires to song. The title's paradoxical self-reference establishes the tone for a series of poems that set forth Queneau's familiar motifs: exorcism of death, various forms of word-play, nocturnal visions, and decrying the fall. Parody is increasingly self-directed in these poems. Having written a significant body of work the poet can, with modest self-assurance, take himself as the object of his own parody and comic barbs. This self-parody expresses a sense of the limits of self and the poet's experience as well as a sense of the limits of language. In self-derision these poems show their consciousness of limits as they mock the aspirations of language to rise to some essential experience—such as a poem.

In "L'Ecole du Troufion" (School for GI's) Queneau muses ironically about his capacity to write when he recalls the doubts he knew during his military training right before World War II: "Suis-je encor soldat ou bien suis-je artiste / Suis-je plutôt gai suis-je plutôt triste" (Am I still a soldier or am I an artist / Am I gay or rather am I sad).[4] To which existential questions an answer of sorts is given when a passing lieutenant screams out, "un surréaliste!" (21). The former surrealist has as many arbitrary identities as there are arbitrary choices for poems. Gratuity is the key, and Queneau capitalizes on the aleatory as the very stuff of his ludic poems. Typical is one called "Ecrit je ne sais pourquoi un quatorze juillet" (Written I don't know why on the fourteenth of July), and another puns bilingually with Queneau's Hamlet complex, in "Etre ou ne pas être Tobie" (To Be or not to Be Tobie). In the fallen world of the absurd, poetry is a gratuitous activity, but a preferred one for, say, making time pass on "hated Sundays": "What to do on this cloudy day / Write a poem perhaps / That has the advantage / Of cultivating fine letters" (69). In short, in many of these playful poems subject matter is subordinated to the often comic workings of the poet's mind, as he muses on the arbitrary choices that will nonetheless offer the "savor of being" when duly noted in "belles lettres" ("Souvenirs," 19).

Queneau is not a poet like his friend Michel Leiris, for whom poetry is a way to live more intensely the experiential world. Queneau is a creator of ironic voices that mimic many points of view, and one reads the presence of the poet as a kind of negative intelligence to whom no single existential stance can be ascribed. In this way Queneau ironically creates, for instance, a voice that calls upon the little birds to come unto him, those little birds whose excrements "make up the charm of Paris, perhaps" ("Encore les pigeons" [Pigeons Again], 118). Parodying his own obsession with pigeons and their droppings, Queneau the poet of the city streets offers a Queneau who recalls days when, rather than being perverted by "grenadine milk" and "electric guitars" youth raised goldfish: "that was far more entertaining / and moral" (119). This constant ironic distance

toward himself finds its ultimate logical development in a poem
about one's self meeting one's self, as a form of "egocentrisme":
"Going around the block / I banged up against myself / Thus can
one in every season / amuse oneself in the extreme" (134). In these
later poems there is little Baudelairean anguish about the self that
must undergo self-scrutiny. Rather this amused self-reflexive stance
is the necessary condition for a kind of tolerance of the world and
all its multifarious appearances, as well as for an acceptance of the
poet's place therein.

There are, however, a number of poems in this collection that
present Queneau's anger about the obvious injustice that man commits in the world. In the expanded edition of *Le Chien à la mandoline*
Queneau includes an homage to Jacques Prévert, and it is clear that
Queneau shares Prévert's indignation and wrath about those forms
of inhumanity that it is the poet's task to denounce. Queneau's
anger is transmuted into a surrealist vision of war in "La Gour-
mande," which is perhaps its most effective form of expression; for
his anger is too cutting in the collection's final poem, "Haute
société" (High society; or, The upper class). In this poem Queneau
denounces the power elite with unrestrained rage, using a litany of
"Très bien" (very fine) to underscore that the "messieurs très bien"
give themselves over to such futile rituals as drinking "cat pipi"
and whiskey.

Queneau's humanism, if such is the proper term, finds its most
powerful expression in *Le Chien à la mandoline* in two major philosophical poems, "Un troublant exploit" and "Ces gouttes de sang."
"Un troublant exploit" (A troubling exploit) portrays Queneau as
a kind of tattered Icarus wanting to flee the world with its "flow
of prisoners" who, with their masks and their images, are too disgustingly like him. More powerful in its restrained expression of
Queneau's anguish about man is "Ces gouttes de sang" (These drops
of blood). The first three stanzas of this poem are a beautifully
controlled neoclassical evocation of the sunrise, the moment when
dawn listens to "screech-owls with weak voices / that tell with
ennui / of the fall into the abyss / of what had come out of it" (88).
The description of dawn may also have a contemporary political
meaning, echoing the metaphor of political revolution conceived as
the "glow in the east," or perhaps dawn is a symbol conveying
optimism about using political power to achieve change.

Man reads in the necessary working of the stars his own hope for necessary revolution or political change:

> Ainsi s'inscrivent dans les astres
> pour les presbytes du futur
> et dogue et duc et leurs désastres
> le sel l'hermès et le sulphur:
> cette signature labile
> est source d'un nouvel espoir

> Thus are written in the stars
> for the farsighted of the future
> and mastiff and duke and their disasters
> the salt Hermes and sulphide
> this unstable signature
> is the origin of a new hope

> (90)

Hermes, the messenger of the gods, is also called Mercury; and the powers of the world—dukes and their mastiffs—find in the vermilion dawn the color of a salt, red mercuric sulphide, a compound known as cinnabar. Cinnabar is one of Queneau's favored compounds, perhaps because it is the central Taoist substance symbolizing the equilibrium of natural forces in the cosmos. But disequilibrium is, as the poem says, eternal, and the arrival of dawn engenders confusion after the moment of hope.

At this moment flies forth an "owl in pasteboard / that famous philosophers / feed with their reason." Owls appear throughout Queneau's poems, in part because they are capable of seeing at night, and in part, as here, because Queneau appears to play with Hegel's claim, in *The Philosophy of Right,* that the owl of Minerva only flies at twilight.[5] By this Hegel meant that philosophy always appears too late, it comes to bring knowledge only after life has undergone the historical changes that philosophy would explain. If this is Hegel's owl in Queneau's fourth stanza, it is a destructive owl, for it stirs up the air and "columns of smoke / bring about with their slag / the inevitable fall *(déchéance)* / of the always renaissant hero" whose drops of blood have been spilled on "this table" (90).

Owls announce being's attempt to overcome nothingness, and they foreshadow the sun-hero's fall into nothingness. One might see here a commentary on the Hegelian vision of the revolutionary hero; or simply Queneau's solar myth describing the inevitable fall of all those who, like Icarus or Phaeton, seek to rise above the limits of the night. Yet, the hero's blood falls on "this table," becoming traces inscribed on the paper of the poem, and in this sense Queneau's poem is a testimony to the cyclical fall of all that exists. Queneau's humanism is a dark, self-conscious transcription of a sense of ultimate failure. And in this self-conscious recording of the mind's failure to surmount nothingness, we might see the perfect example of Queneau's anti-Hegelian Hegelianism.

To turn to the *Sonnets* that our doggy poet proposes is to turn to something like another series of exercises in style. Since the sonnet's invention in the thirteenth century it has become the most codified and probably the most practiced of poetic genres. For the twentieth-century writer it is perhaps impossible to write sonnets that do not burlesquely reflect upon that tradition. In his sonnets Queneau harks back to the poetic tradition of French Renaissance writers as well as to sonnets of the early seventeenth century, to poems by Saint-Amant or Voiture—with an occasional nod to Mallarmé. Queneau's sonnets are sometimes philosophically serious works, but, more often, they play humorously with the reader's expectation as to what the sonnet should be. Parodies of diction and burlesque subject matter abound. He can even create an untranslatable bit of nonsense that seems to generate meaning merely because it is cast in the sonnet form:

> Acriborde acromate et marneuse la vague
> au bois des écumés brouillés de mille cleurs
> pulsereuse choisit un destin coquillague
> sur le nable où les nrous nretiennent les nracleus
>
> (139)

Just as Queneau's sonnets propose to offer burlesque or mock heroic renderings of the logic of the sonnet, here signifiers are teasingly deformed so that they offer a burlesque version of French—and non-French—phonemes. This is parody to at least the second or third degree, not unlike what Queneau's contemporary Michaux has done.

Queneau's sonnets provide another comic feast for the reader who wants to follow a supremely intelligent mind as it converts any subject matter into a game based on the rules of a traditional literary form. There has of course always been a ludic side to writing sonnets, since the sonnet is generated by mathematically defined game rules with regard to length and prosody. This highly codified ludic aspect of the sonnet form perhaps explains why Queneau used it again in his *Cent mille milliards de poèmes (One Hundred Million Million Poems)* in 1961. Taken as a totality this work offers the reader an aleatory text that has an upper mathematical limit for the number of poems that the reader can "create" by combining lines from different poems among themselves. In some ways this extraordinary work redefines what the random might be in literature. For this "collection" Queneau wrote ten sonnets, each having fourteen lines that are complete in themselves as units of meaning. He then placed the ten sonnets together sequentially, one atop the other, cut each one so that the reader can open the fourteen lines of each poem and combine the lines of all the poems freely. This combinative freedom allows the reader to compose a sonnet with lines from any of the ten sonnets, giving him the mathematical possibility of $10^{14}$ sonnets, or one hundred thousand billion poems. The mind must strain a bit when beholding this little book, with its strange format of dangling lines, to realize that one could read it twenty-four hours a day for a lifetime and never exhaust it. Yet there is a finite number of possibilities for the combinative system as determined simply by the binding that holds the lines in place on the left side of the volume. And to the inevitable question, "Are they interesting poems?" we can only answer that masterworks may lurk within, but it would probably require a literate computer to find them—a project that in a somewhat different form has interested Oulipo.

In sessions of the Ouvroir de littérature potentielle, Queneau and his mathematically minded friends continued throughout the sixties and seventies to experiment with various kinds of texts and new game constraints for the production of texts. Little of this is apparent, however, in the three collections of poems that Queneau published in the sixties: *Courir les rues* (Running in the streets), *Battre la campagne* (Scouring the countryside), and *Fendre les flots* (Cutting through the waters). Using three clichés for his titles Queneau signaled that this significant renewal of his poetic practice was neither avant-garde nor experimental in nature. Taken together the three volumes could be likened to concentric circles—formed by town, country, and sea—proposing a kind of cosmology that one might glean from daily experience. Not the least of those experiences is the experience of what language says about these three

regions, language in the form of clichés or language taken from the
innumerable sources that go to make up what we can say about
town, country, and sea, or in short, the world.

Most typically the city poems of the first collection, *Courir les
rues,* unfold as promenades, as walks through Paris, or, to use a
word that recalls both Baudelaire and Apollinaire, as *flâneries* that
bring the ambulant poet into contact with the city's destiny. As in
Queneau's early works, the meaning of time and history for Paris,
the archetypical city, is destruction and metamorphosis. The city's
disappearance can be, if not retarded, at least mediated by language,
which Queneau borrows from literature, history books, or, frequently, from the *Guide Bleu,* Queneau's favored guide to what is
and what was in Paris. The *Guide Bleu* makes the cityscape speak.
The poet need at times only arrange the guidebook's language in
free verse form such as when he wanders blindly in a pitch black
church and learns from the guide that "it was constructed in nineteen
hundred and three / by an architect named Lucien Roy / and that
the edifice is 'above all' illuminated / by the glassed cupola / above
the transept crossing. . . ."[6] To which prosaic information the
unseeing poet can only add that "this is to have of lighting a
concept / lacking in severity." Language and reality do not always
mesh.

In many of these poems Queneau uses the most prosaic language
in a refusal of lyricism. He prefers to incorporate literally in them
the language that the city yields, often as a kind of "ready-made"
art form, to recall Marcel Duchamp; or as a kind of play with pop
forms of language that recall the work of a pop artist like Andy
Warhol. The ready-made side is most clearly demonstrated when
Queneau, using a Baudelaire concordance, constructs a collage of
lines about Paris taken literally from Baudelaire's poems (complete
with the concordance line number). The pop side also involves the
quotation of preexisting language, such as one can read in the streets,
in advertising: "Au sommet la gaine Scandale / Tabou Crylor Tabou
Tergal / tourisme italien Cinzano / Porto blanc et rouge Porto /
machines à laver Ignis" (At the top Scandal girdles / Tabou Crylor
Tabou Tergal / Italian Tourism Cinzano / White Porto and red
Porto / Ignis washing machines, 112). Read against this list the
irony of the epigraph to *Courir les rues,* taken from Heraclitus,
becomes apparent. Quoting his favored Greek to the effect that
"there, too, there are gods," Queneau seems to imply that it is in

the marketplace that we find the language of our deities, the language of the commercial city that modernists like Mallarmé saw as unfit for poetic usage. But, as we shall see, girdles are always for Queneau a symbol of culture's highest aspirations.

Using a catalog as the organizing principle for a poem has become something of a tradition, beginning perhaps with Apollinaire and carried on in France by Jacques Prévert (to whom Queneau pays homage in the "inventory" given by "Le Paris de Paroles"—the Paris of words or *Paroles,* Prévert's most famous collection). Queneau adds his own twist to the poem-inventory by seeking, often nostalgically, to endow it with a historical dimension, though his lists usually demonstrate *al contrario* how little history is to be gleaned from his walks. Starting at the "Hôtel Hilton" the poet takes a stroll and ends up with a list of things that no longer exist in Paris: "dans cette région qu'il y avait le Veldive / totalement escamoté / c'est aussi dans le coin qu'habitait l'extralucide / dont parle André Breton dans Nadja / elle s'appelait madame Sacco" (in this neighborhood was the Winter Sports Palace / totally gone today / also around here lived the clairvoyant / that André Breton talks about in Nadja / she was called madame Sacco, 51). Adding reminiscences, historical and literary, to his lists, Queneau lets the random experience of the past enter the poem in what becomes a kind of aleatory vision of the transient.

For nothing exists except the relentless present, onto which the poet projects a past. The emblem of this absolute reign of the present is given by the way a painting exists, like Delacroix's painting of Jacob and the angel in the Saint Sulpice church. This story from the mythic past of the Book of Genesis exists as the fixed present moment that the artist once created, but the painted struggle continues in a continuous present that will know no end—until the "immense old building" falls down ("Genèse XXXII, 24," 64). The future is inscribed in the present as an eventual fall, even for buildings of "Grand Standigne" (High class) with their plexiglass, garbage disposals, and antennae, that will necessarily age "du poids infini de la tristesse des choses" (with the infinite weight of the sadness of things, 70). Things, it is true, are everywhere, and it is the task of the melancholy Gnostic streetsweeper, like the Parisian municipal sweepers from Martinique, to scoop them from the gutter, though the poet can do nothing with them except let them enter into the poem: "crottes de chiens vieilles lettres / mégots bâtonnets

de sucettes / épingle à cheveux verre brisé" (dog dung old letters /
cigarette butts lollipop sticks / hair pins broken glass, 77). The
urban landscape accedes to language in all its fallen state, for Queneau, to coin an expression that would apply to much contemporary
art, is an artist in junk.

A good many of the poems in *Courir les rues* express a direct vision,
mediated through language, of what the *flâneur* sees in Parisian
streets. In *Battre la campagne,* however, Queneau's poems present
country scenes that exist primarily as they are codified in language.
To be sure Queneau presents scenes taken from the countryside of
the sixties, but it was rapidly disappearing then as urban areas spread
throughout the land. Much of the comedy in these poems derives
from the contrast between our conventional notions about the country and the reality of an urbanized landscape that is hardly bucolic.

In many of these poems Queneau explores the various semantic
fields, the various regions of our lexicon, that go to make up what
we mean by "country"—a region that is often defined largely by
its opposition to what we mean by "city." (And this opposition is
perhaps more pointed in French than in English.) Queneau contrasts
the contemporary countryside, with its automobiles, factories, television sets, and transistors, with conventional lexes about rurality,
especially as taken from poets such as La Fontaine or Ronsard, or
from proverbs and legends, as well as from the usual clichés about
rural life. Much of this play is, however, a purely linguistic work
that owes little to the poet's direct vision: one has difficulty imagining Queneau frolicking in pastoral bliss.

One of Queneau's strategies for staging these ironic bucolics is
to use conventional types of characters in the creation of brief dramatic scenes. We encounter the woodsman and the peasant, the
shepherd and the blacksmith, as well as the city dweller on holiday
or in retirement. Queneau also gives us a good many personified
animals and forces of nature: owls, flies, spiders, birds, trees, storms,
and lightning. These various "characters" function as actors in a
composite portrait of what one means by "country life" in conventional terms, though these portrayals also present a comedy of types.
This comedy turns frequently on a deflection from our conventional
expectations. Queneau's gardener spends his time "vituperating cats"
that drop their dung in his garden ("Maigre engrais" or "Thin
Fertilizer," 141). One of his peasants goes to the city, but not to
visit a city cousin: he prefers the Crazy Horse Saloon after spending

the afternoon studying his genealogy at the National Library ("Le Paysan à la ville" [The peasant in town], 168). Or, in a reversal of a familiar proverb a bishop kicks a dog in order to demonstrate the emptiness of proverbs, especially one showing all may get along in this world. ("L'évêque et le chien" [The bishop and the dog], 202).

Queneau's sympathy goes out to all forms of life, such as the humble slug that ventures forth, needing our affection so that its anguish may diminish, as well as its slobber, which covers *les soucis*— worries or marigolds in this play on words (197). Queneau's poetic universe is imbued with a sense of innocence, not unlike a child's world, that Queneau offers with ironic variations. His sympathy with a slug is one example; it is also complementary to his ambition in a number of poems to rewrite La Fontaine's fables. This rewriting consists in comically reversing these classical fables so that they no longer dramatize a kind of "realist" doctrine describing the primacy of brute power and the necessity of constant lucidity if the weak and innocent are not to be devoured by the strong. In Queneau's version of the fable about the lamb and the wolf, the lamb beats up the wolf and then victoriously "pisses in the $H_2O$ of the pure stream" (127). In his portrayal of La Fontaine's ant, the prudent insect falls off a blade of grass, but is gently received into the arms of the grasshopper, who, in place of "alpine sports" like grass climbing, recommends that they take up dances such as the bourrée or the Brasilian *matchiche* (122). This dialectical whimsy, reversing a received literary model, is a supremely civilized form of play. It also opens up new spaces for writing what we might mean by "country." Certainly Queneau intends in these texts to create a space, existing under the sign of innocence, in which our received notions about the world, codified in literature or in clichés, are scrutinized with playful irony.

In counterpoint to innocence recurs Queneau's obsession with universal erosion under whose sign he places the entire collection by opening it with the poem "L'usure"—meaning the wear and decline that affects all. The poet notes, "Death is also vegetable" (132), but the bucolic world is, in addition, the place where the observer can find affirmation of the cycles of being that may annul time and the destruction it brings. Like a Taoist sage, "under the flower- / ing of civilized trees," he can look for the suspension of the illusory flow of time: "Adieu Adieu La vie tranquille / se déplace vers le passé / Peut-être un futur immobile / me la fera retrouver"

(Adieu Adieu The quiet life / moves toward the past / Perhaps an immobile future / will cause me to find it again, 120–21). Yet beyond despair about erosion or faint hopes for the abolition of time lies mystery. It is the mystery that one is forced to acknowledge when one strips oneself of all pretensions to knowledge and, like the "country traveler," recognizes that one understands nothing about the enormous number of things that simply are (144). The disabused intelligence must cry out in recognizing its limits, and these limits become readily apparent when one tries to categorize the bucolic world of nature. Queneau had no absolute faith in language, with its multitudinous categories for what is, for slugs and lightning, farmers and spiders, oak trees and dogs; and these poems point to a skepticism that was receptive to contemplating mysteries in silence.

Queneau's third volume in this trilogy, *Fendre les flots,* is perhaps his most successfully sustained masterwork. It shares many of the ironic and comic traits that characterize the two preceding collections, but it is more single-minded in its unified poetic project: to explore the web of interrelating metaphors that can be generated by words and concepts such as sea, ocean, water, and streams, as well as related notions such as travel, ships, and maritime life. The sea and the semantic fields related to it offer one of the great stocks of recurrent metaphors that underwrite the Western poetic and philosophical tradition. The combinatory possibilities of these metaphors are enormous and can express virtually all that poets and thinkers have said about time and memory, life and death, or being and nothingness. Who, after Heraclitus, can bend his mind sufficiently *not* to conceive of time as a river? In their power as all-encompassing metaphors, the sea, water, and streams can also fold back upon themselves, designating themselves as metaphors, in a self-reflexive web in which every metaphor can relate to every other. In writing the poet must "cut through the waves" of his own words:

> Presser la mer des histoires
> dans un filet finement tressé
> actes, actes méritoires
> qui mènent au feu sacré

> To press out of the sea stories
> into a finely tressed net

> acts, meritorious acts
> that lead to the sacred fire
> (247)

This is a dialectical understanding that knows that one metaphor can always give rise to its opposite, in the play of language that can go from water to fire, or from the immanent to the transcendent.

The movement toward the sea begins, in the first poems in the collection, in the city. It begins, not surprisingly, in the gutter, for the small streams that collect there sweep away the debris of the city's daily dissolution and carry its detritus to rivers and finally to the purifying ocean: "The great devouring sea digests the residues / all the garbage cans of all the cities of all the continents" (228). Especially in the opening poems, but also throughout the book, one encounters the leitmotiv of purgation and purification. Queneau views the sea as "incorruptible" (311), a source of cleansing surrounded by the pure sands of the circumambiant beaches. Queneau is obviously not addressing ecological concerns in *Fendre les flots*. Rather, he is, perhaps to his own great solace, celebrating a mythic realm created by the metaphors of our culture according to which, as Saint John-Perse says in his poem *Amers,* the ocean is always begun again. The sea embodies the principle of eternal beginnings and the renewal of being.

One can make plausible and real connections for seeing spittle travel from the gutter to the ocean, but Queneau is equally as interested in the plausible and sometimes implausible semantic connections he can find in exploring these images of water. If the poet is exploring the (concept of) sea, then he may, as poet, liken himself to a boat or a navigator—an image Queneau had already used in his psychological explorations in *Chêne et chien.* But in probing these metaphors the poet can also follow other semantic directions and see himself as a fish, a shrimp, or a cephalopod such as a cuttlefish that emits, like the poet, his ink into and on the sea (243). In this interconnecting series of metaphors, the poet-voyager travels on a metaphysical sea where he sees that the trip takes place for each passenger alone, in search of some realm beyond the limits of metaphor: "as for the solitary passenger, unique / he looks upon all this tragic domain / with a rather indifferent eye / always remains on the beach / the elements of a simple dream / for one who is dead or living" (252).

Metaphorical transference allows Queneau to transform aquatic flora and fauna into characters in small poetic dramas—though the self-referential nature of many of Queneau's metaphors tend to transform these dramas into allegories about the poem itself. The poet addresses, for instance, a warning to *coquillages,* to shellfish that they would do well to avoid beaches where "heavy bipeds" may eat them and then listen to their shells to hear the sound of the sea—which is what one "hears" in reading the poems of *Fendre les flots.* This kind of poem seems to move in its utter simplicity between a paradoxical Taoist allegory and a simple meditation on the hazards of existence. Or in a few lines Queneau describes the voyage of a spider, blown by the winds across the oceans, passing by migratory birds and flying fish, and concludes that "au bout de son fil l'araignée / impassible continue" (on the end of its thread the spider / impassive goes on, 241). These exercises in descriptive concision suggest paradoxes and resonances that seem to want to open up on some realm of silence beyond the limits of metaphor and language. The dialectical exercises of Parmenides or of the Taoist Chuang Tzu stand as models for this kind of demonstration that any statement can suggest its opposite and is therefore inadequate for any purpose other than demonstrating its own inadequacy. Queneau's poems frequently enact litotic dramas of paradox or suggestion in order to convey a sense of a possible transcendence of language, though Queneau's comic sense of his own limitations never allows him to move toward a positive exposition of what might otherwise seem a kind of poetic mysticism.

The poems of *Fendre les flots* also seek to represent the world of childhood, though the child's experience is now refracted through the viewpoint of the aging poet. In this sense polar opposites of infancy and old age are often compressed into the same poem. This recall of childhood is motivated by the poet's remembrance that it was during his early years that he discovered the metaphorical capacities of the sea, of the power of words and images of the ocean to capture his imagination. There is undoubtedly a great deal of autobiography in Queneau's remembrance of how books transformed the sea for the child, even more powerfully than did actual excursions in boats or rambles by the seaside. For "L'enfant qui grandit" (The child growing up) his cradle is already a sailing vessel. Later the schoolboy looks at maps in books and, with no thought of ever really sailing, dreams of cities like Galveston and Tampico (though one may suspect this child has already read Apollinaire's evocation of such ports). And above all the boy reads, neglecting his school-books, the "Livre relié de rouge où la mer des histoires / fait rouler têtes et mains sous les flots conquérants" (Book bound in red where the sea of stories / makes heads and hands roll under the victorious waves, 287). He becomes a "dry land sailor" by exploring the dictionary, that book of interrelating terms and potential metaphors. The dictionary first offers him the image of the three-masted ship upon which he can embark in his imagination. Unlike the Baudelairean poet of "The Voyage" who finds that the world of books is no longer equal to the child's appetite for life, Queneau finds in himself an *homme-gamin,* a man-child still capable of both exulting in and feeling pain before the infinite variety of words and the world: "Où donc court cet homme adulte / cet homme mûr ce gamin / s'il voit ceci il exulte / s'il voit cela il est chagrin / il est vieux par le babillage / il est jeune comme un perclus" (Where is this adult man running / this mature man this kid / if he sees this he exults / if he sees that he's sad / he is old in his babbling / he's young like a cripple, 312).

The metaphors of sea, river, and water bring about *chagrin,* metaphysical sadness in Queneau's case, about their capacity to signify the self and the world's flight, disappearance, and intransience. The tides of Brittany produce the electricity that allows one to read the printed page; but their cyclical destruction of the coast allows one to read the tides as part of a cycle of giving birth to debris ("Les Marées" [The tides], 234). Metaphors of water and waves are founding metaphors that allow one to read death dialectically against the permanence of the sea, for waves, like the self, have no stability. And in this network of metaphors the poet must ask what he finds that is stable, what is really his, against the backdrop of water's literal and metaphorical unceasing change ("Ces mois" [These months], 234).

*Fendre les flots* is finally an interrogative work, questioning the nature of a self that can only be conceived in terms of a received metaphorical register of codified images. If we think of the self in terms of continuity and discontinuity, or depths and surface, we are using images describing rivers and the sea; and yet is it possible to conceive our own identity other than in these terms? There appear to be no evident answers to the questions these poems pose, although that does not prevent Queneau from asking explicit questions, often at the conclusion of the poems, that vibrate with both anguish and an ironic serenity about the simple state of being and having been. This interrogation of his identity underlies Queneau's fascination with images and objects of maritime provenance, such as, say, relics like a pair of nautical binoculars left by a relative of the Victorian era who sailed about the world: "Les grands livres noirs de bord / ont disparu je ne sais quand / mais les jumelles toujours présentes / permettent de voir quoi? de voir quoi?" (The big black logbooks / disappeared I don't know when / but the ever present binoculars / allow you to see what? to see what?, 279). Direct vision of the past, even of one's own past, is impossible, and the interrogative mode seems finally to be the only one available to the poet who faces his stock of metaphors as a kind of closure from within which he must write or be silent.

This sense of language's closure is part of Queneau's acute sense of limits. It also stands behind his refusal of the possibility of poetic originality: Creation always takes place within the combinatory possibilities that language allows. There is an ethical side to this recognition of limits that serves as a prelude to Queneau's final collection, *Morale élémentaire*. Recognizing originality to be an illusion, the poet comes to see freedom as something to be won through an acknowledgment that repetition is fundamental to existence. In "Se libérer" (Liberate oneself, 268) he first posits that, though man can easily recognize the noisy chains that bind him, there are forms of bondage that operate silently. Man hears the clanking of metal chains, but "rarely does he discern the silent hold of the algae" (77). The ocean, both literally and figuratively it would seem, can teach the limits the recognition of which can liberate man: "S'il entendait mieux cependant / ce que raconte la tempête / il apprendrait de l'océan / quelle longe il porte en sa tête" (If he listened better however / to what the storm tells / he would learn from the ocean / what a tether he carries within his head, 77). The slow working of algae is a concrete emblem of necessary natural cycles, as is the recurrence of the storm. With these emblems Queneau suggests a meditative way of gaining freedom, in a nearly stoic or Epicurean sense. Man must bring his inner world into harmony with the unity of being, and this harmony can be thought through the language of poetry and its recurrent metaphors. The sea is always present as the image, the emblem, and the word that allow us to think our way of being in the world.

The moral concerns of *Fendre les flots* are not transparent in Queneau's last work, although it is explicitly called *Morale élémentaire* (Elementary ethics, or Basic treatise on morals). Nor is it certain that *poetry* is the best term for this writing. In opening this volume after reading Queneau's earlier work, readers will feel at the very least that they have changed poetic universes, since Queneau's last collection of texts can give the impression that one is reading the *I Ching* as rewritten by Gertrude Stein. In a sense it is. The book is certainly Queneau's most hermetic work (as testifies the wide range of commentary given to it by a seminar of Queneau specialists that lasted for two years in Paris). The book resists any easy interpretation, for a kind of indeterminate ambiguity is one of the principles of writing that these texts put into play. Most critics agree that Queneau freely used Chinese models for much of the writing, both for forms and themes, but there is no consensus about Queneau's intent in playing these intertextual games. Some would claim this is Queneau's greatest work; others have doubts.

*Morale élémentaire* is certainly another cosmological work, and it can be read against *Petite cosmogonie portative*. For it refuses the logic of causal development that underwrites evolutionary thought. In the most general terms this refusal of logical connections and linear development reflects the modes of thought found in classical Chinese cosmology (such as the refusal to think abstractly of objects as substances that can be logically defined in terms of their individual elements). One's first impression of *Morale élémentaire* is that the texts operate in terms of radical discontinuity, though discontinuity presupposes abstract and discrete elements that can be potentially joined together. Perhaps it would be better to say that *Morale élémentaire* proposes a vision of constant mutation in which all is related to all as mobile forms manifesting themselves in transient groupings under the sway of some cosmic totality or unity. This kind of cosmological writing would find analogies in the Taoist vision of the all as a uniform tissue of movement and change—with the observer, unlike the classical observer of Western science, integrated into the tissue. The key to this lies in cycles of change in which "before and after follow each other," as the *Tao te Ching* puts it, with reference to being as a ring. The function of *The Book of Changes,* also called the *I Ching,* the classical Chinese work to which Queneau constantly alludes in the third part, is not only to predict the cycles of nature; it is also to comment on the harmonious nature of these

changes. Systematic thought and linear causal relations have no place
in understanding these changes, for, as Marcel Granet says in his
classic study of Chinese civilization, "The idea of mutation does
away with any philosophical interest in an inventory of nature by
which one could propose to set forth a series of facts by distinguishing
antecedents and their consequences."[7]

With these general remarks in mind one can open *Morale élémentaire* and also find a very contemporary example of recent French
*écriture* or self-conscious writing that aims at producing a largely
nonreferential text. I would suggest that Queneau set out in this
work to show younger French writers and theorists of *écriture* what
a self-contained text could be, especially one playing with Chinese
models of thought. One might recall that Jean-Luc Godard's film
*La Chinoise* was emblematic of the sixties' Maoist mode in France,
a kind of intellectual fashion that can also be associated with the
review *Tel Quel* and its editor-novelist Philippe Sollers. In a work
such as *Nombres* (Numbers, 1968) Sollers, for example, had pretensions of using Chinese models to bring about a cultural revolution
in Paris, if not in Western rationality. I shall contend that Queneau's
novel *The Flight of Icarus* (1968) was something of a parody of novels
by younger French novelists who had been writing "New Novels."
In the same perspective *Morale élémentaire* would be a reaction to the
then current French intellectual scene, not through parody, but
through an elaborate demonstration of how a modern Western mind,
one that had meditated on Chinese literature for forty years, could
actually rewrite the world with a Chinese grid.

Obviously the "morals" of Queneau's work are different from the
pop revolutionary praxis that Godard's students or *Tel Quel* writers
wanted to find in modern China. This "elementary lesson in ethics"
that Queneau offers the seventies had nothing to do with the necessity of violently transforming thought and hence the world.
Whatever be the ironic dimension of Queneau's intent—and his
bemused use of models of prophecy in his novels suggests there is
a great deal of irony in his choice to rewrite a Chinese work of
fortunetelling—these ethics turn on a contemplative understanding
of the cosmic stage.

*Morale élémentaire* offers three approaches to writing in its three
sections. The first part consists of fifty-two poems having a verse
form that Queneau invented. It would appear that Queneau rather
liberally adapted here the medieval Chinese lyric form known as the

Tz'u. This form allowed both colloquial and bookish diction; moreover, in omitting lines that contained verbs it often used "lines consisting of a series of noun phrases which build up an elegant picture and produce what might be called a 'pointillistic effect.' "[8] Queneau's pictures may not be judged elegant, but they are pointillistic. The poems in the first part possess a pointillistic harshness that, in its starkness, also recalls the later texts of Samuel Beckett.

Let us offer an example of this unique form by quoting one poem in its entirety:

| Main sourde | Main gourde | Main lourde |
|---|---|---|
| | Main expectatrice | |
| Main traceuse | Main traceuse | Main traceuse |
| | Main dessinatrice | |
| Encre fluide | Machines voletantes | Papiers éblouis |
| | | |
| | Main scriptrice | |
| | Les cygnes | |
| | d'aujourd'hui | |
| | ignorants | |
| | ignifient | |
| | le lac argenté | |
| | de feux | |
| | et de signes | |
| | | |
| Échelle posée | Sel tombant | Chat passant |
| | Main protectrice | |

Deaf hand   Numbed hand   Heavy hand / Expecting Hand / Tracing hand Tracing hand Tracing hand / Designing hand / Fluid ink Fluttering machines Dazzled pages / Scripting hand / The swans / today / ignorant / set on fire / the silver lake / of fire / and of signs / Ladder put down / Falling salt / Passing cat / Protective hand[9]

Each poem in the first part follows this pattern. Beginning with three lines composed of substantives and adjectives, each of which is followed by a noun and an adjective that seem almost to be a résumé of the preceding line, the poem then sets forth seven lines having syntactic connections. This semantically unified series is then followed by another line of substantives and adjectives and a finale of one noun and adjective. It seems quite likely that with this form Queneau was attempting to capture something of the iconic sense that Chinese poetry possesses in the spacing of its calligraphy. The

form is arresting as a visual unfolding and, according to some of
Queneau's critics, allows one to read the words in various orders,
without regard for the normal conventions of Western typography
and the reading order that this typography imposes. Whatever may
be the liberating effect these poems have with regard to linear order,
they generate meaning through a kind of cluster effect, especially
through recurrent motifs that can suggest internal associations with
other motifs in the text. Queneau also brings in intertextual associations with his other writings, as well as with the writings of a
good bit of the Western canon.

In the poem we have just quoted the word *hand,* for example, is
associated with the act of writing. Through this association it is
linked with other self-referential motifs in *Morale élémentaire* that
designate the work's own genesis and, perhaps through its genesis,
the coming to be of the world itself. Language passing through the
writing hand begets a cosmos (a viewpoint that makes of Queneau,
one might add, a very occidental Oriental). Other intertextual workings of the poems are shown in this particular text by the allusion
to Mallarmé. Queneau seems to rewrite the sonnet "The lively,
lovely, and virginal today" in which Mallarmé's *cygne-signe* (swan-
sign) has been frozen in a lake that refuses it freedom to know
transcendence. Queneau's swans, ignorant of Mallarmé's, burn in
an image of cosmic renewal, more phoenix than swan, as they set
the lake on fire—presumably this is the sense of the neologism
*ignifier,* deriving from the Latin *ignis* or "fire."

The final nouns in this poem are somewhat obscure, though the
associations of ladders, cats, bad luck, and throwing salt for pro-
tection suggest various popular superstitions. It would certainly not
be beyond Queneau's capacity for irony to associate writing and
superstitious practices as perhaps equally vain practices for deter-
mining the outcome of cosmic events. There are a good many such
jokes throughout *Morale élémentaire,* though one must hasten to add
that the dominant tonality throughout the poems of the first part
is grisaille: Queneau creates a monochromatic sense of the flowing
of days and nights, of the unrelieved cycle of seasons in rain and
snow, in which one perpetually finds that "It is quite dark / beneath
the ribs / of an umbrella" (25). Clouds are omnipresent, intertextual
signs alluding as much to Baudelaire's impossible desire to escape
with them as to their status as the favored Taoist image of mutations.
And as very Parisian clouds they keep the gutters in constant activity.

As these few examples show, Queneau's semantic play in these poems sets up an overdetermination of interpretative possibilities that is matched, syntactically, by an underdetermination as to how one may combine elements. This combinative freedom allows one to associate freely, to produce meanings without normal syntactic and semantic constraints; but it can also leave one in doubt as to what to do with many words. This problem of indetermination is even greater in the work's second part, consisting of a series of prose pieces that seem a prelude to Queneau's specifically rewriting the *I Ching* in the third part. However, these texts are partially unified in their concern again with the act of writing and reading. The first piece offers an ironic image of the reader in its first line: "Le quêteur trébuche dans les marais" (The quester / alms-collector stumbles in the swamp, 63). The quest and collecting (for meaning perhaps) lead through a series of textual permutations that culminate in the final piece's evocation of nature, with descriptions of earth, mountain, forest, still waters, running waters, and the final one-word reference to the sky that opens onto the third part. If there is any total unity to *Morale élémentaire,* perhaps it is to be found in the passage that runs from the earth, as described in the first part's dark poems, through the quest of the second part, to open finally onto heaven and the play of the cosmos in part three. The polarity of heaven and earth has many antecedents, in both Greek and Chinese cosmology, and this notion of a unifying, yet discordant coexistence of cosmic opposites can describe the way *Morale élémentaire* functions as a whole.

In the second part the clearest prose piece would be the third text, which provides a metacommentary on the workings of the poem at this point:

Why do these lines change? They are imprinted with force and their tracery seems indelible. The child is busy with stamps, plants, pebbles. One curve is accentuated, another is effaced. He is at the head of his class. He is at the bottom of his class. There's another one that's just born and begins to trace out its way. He is sent to war. Others are mixed together. So many things happen in these illiterate writings *(écritures analphabètes).* And what a surprise to see new furrows dug out. Even white hair finds an echo there. So many mysteries, you can really say that. So many mysteries. (65)

The text mixes together references to itself and its "mysteries" with references to the writer, as child and as old man, though certain lines seem to apply ambiguously to either text or writer. The writing of self and the writing itself are conflated here in an ambiguous play of reference. This ambiguity perhaps constitutes a semantic "purgatory" on the way from earth to heaven.

Other texts in part 2 lend themselves to this interpretation, especially the ninth text with its specific allusion to Dante and Virgil in purgatory. The search for writing, self, and the way to heaven exists largely in the interrogative mode in the second part, as one sees in Queneau's question about Dante's passage to paradise. The travelers of the ninth text—Dante the quester and his guide Virgil—"would compose a beautiful staging for an allegorical morality play, that could be explained to anyone, but in what theater could you stage it?" (71). Other texts take on contrastive values with this questioning of textual goals. The tenth piece alludes to the Chinese conception of space as a square, whereas the twelfth text deals with the notion of time as circular. Nature seems affirmed as perduring presence here, especially in the texts describing the cycles of things. In contrast to nature are history and the use men make of history: "When the centuries are ground up they furnish a kind of powder that is good for the combat of doctrines" (77). The movement toward heaven leaves history in its wake as a self-effacing illusion—though the "centuries remain inscribed somewhere on some grain of sand" (77).

The second section ends when it opens up onto heaven, that realm that includes all things, and is assigned the number 3 by the numerology of the *I Ching*. The third section of *Morale élémentaire* contains sixty-four texts, the same number as the number of hexagrams (or *koua*, the cosmic cycles) of the Chinese work of divination. The reader who has enough patience to compare each of Queneau's prose pieces with the corresponding hexagram and commentary in the *I Ching* will find that in nearly all cases (or, with sufficient ingenuity, perhaps in all cases) Queneau makes allusion to either the hexagram or to some of the commentary that has grown up around this work originally compiled in the fifth century B. C. Queneau has not, of course, merely translated this work of prophetic numerology, for the relation of his texts to the hexagrams often involves ironic reversals and comic amplifications of motifs in the Chinese work. One might say that the *I Ching* provides a scaffolding upon which Queneau constructs his texts, using a fair amount of borrowed building material.

This borrowed material evokes the ten thousand things that Chinese cosmology proposes as the totality of what is and which we might call the beginning of ten thousand intertextual allusions. Let us offer a concrete example by quoting the third text:

> The idea of the poem lies in the cloud. Down below the poet who thought that he could breathe with ease realizes that his bronchi are stuffed up. He coughs. What a cough! Everything resounds with this cough. He grows red from embarrassment, his blood flows a bit more rapidly. Thoracic thunder shakes the foggy sky. Now words are traced on the white sheet of paper. Is this the beginning of a collection *(recueil)?* In any case it should contain ten thousand things. It's still just a project. (85)

The poem is in the clouds, a recurrent Taoist emblem for the artist's task, for he must trace the clouds and capture the lines of force that constitute the mobility of the way of things. Beneath these Oriental clouds stands a Western poet whose infirmities resonate throughout his world, the world that the text is becoming. This conflating of the Tao and autobiography gives rise to the text, which is to say, to this cosmos that resounds with the poet's own cough. The questioning marks the text's consciousness of its own beginnings as well as the existential doubts that arise at the beginning of a creative project. And if one consults the third hexagram of the *I Ching* one finds that it describes in effect the difficulty encountered at the outset of projects—under the sign of clouds and thunder.

These sixty-four texts function on different registers as they often playfully enjoin us to heed the combinations and mutations of the ten thousand things. Queneau joins motifs from *The Book of Changes* with allusions to himself and to his personal history to create seemingly arbitrary vignettes that nonetheless propose emblematic moments in the cycle of being. These are the writings of an older man for whom the ultimate moral is, as Taoist sages held, that life and death are illusory aspects of the great harmony of what is. The poet nearing death knows that "the fête now finished, the visitor goes away, carrying off his memories" (138). But if "all declines," the cycle also demands that suddenly one day there is "a zinnia flowering and a dazzling anemone" (94).

It would undoubtedly be too simple to say that in *Morale élémentaire* Queneau finally brought about a reconciliation between himself and the cosmos. Perhaps one might modify this judgment by saying that in this final poetic work Queneau created a work whose movement aims at divesting the world of any sense of the fall. The first part, with its dark repetitions, offers the "earth," the realm where history and myth, the autobiographical and the quotidian, are mixed in a writing that is still nostalgic for the paradise that, to return to where we began this discussion of poetry, Queneau defined as the absent space from which, like Vlaminck, every artist works. The passage from earth to heaven leads to often whimsical texts of cosmic change that offer a play of repetition no longer cursed by the weight of the fall. In the final text of *Morale élémentaire,* or "Before Completion," as the sixty-fourth hexagram of the *I Ching* is called, time is no longer the measure of decadence, but rather "le parcours accompli"—"the distance traversed." The end approaches: "To get there it will have been necessary to move heaven and earth" (146). In résumé, then, Queneau's *Morale élémentaire* is the measure of the poet's effort to move from earth to heaven and finally deny the fall.

*Morale élémentaire* is Queneau's literary testament, especially for its demonstration of the high stakes that Queneau saw involved in the practice of poetry. Like the Chinese, Queneau saw in poetry a civilizing activity, though, in our view, Queneau's Orientalism afforded him an approach to poetry by which he might renew the Western neoclassical tradition—while avoiding the Christian sense of guilt that impregnates that tradition. With his Orientalism he wished to forge a self-reflexive poetics of innocence, of language freely accepted as the basis of culture and civilization without guilt; in short, a poetics of language and culture as the play of what is.

To conclude our discussion of Queneau's poetry, we stress that it is important to see throughout Queneau's work his attachment to the neoclassical tradition. One can conveniently define this tradition as one inaugurated by Horace, continued by Dante and Boileau, and renewed by modernists such as Ezra Pound and James Joyce. Neoclassicism makes of the poetic use of language a founding institution for civilization. Horace, and Boileau after him, describe the writer's task when they portray the poet Orpheus as the tamer of nature and the musician Amphion as the builder of cities. Queneau's Orpheus is inscribed throughout his work in the image of the poet as the modest and often ironic self-deprecating writer who plays at rejuvenating culture thorugh festive parody.

Like Horace, and much like Ezra Pound, Queneau quite firmly believed that the task of poetry, as a work of civilization, was to renew language and keep it alive. This point of view is quite explicit in his essays in *Volontés,* written in the thirties; and it underlies many of the poems that make up his *ars poetica.* Thus, in a poem from *Le Chien à la mandoline* having the revealing title "La chair chaude des mots" (The warm flesh of words), he enjoins us: "Prends ces mots dans tes mains et sens leurs pieds agiles / Et sens leur coeur qui bat comme celui du chien" (Take these words in your hands and feel their agile feet / And feel their heart that beats like a dog's, 193). To understand poetry one must first recognize the fragility of words and the care they need if they are to "live" in any full sense. There is an organic view of language behind this poetics, one going back at least to Horace's comparing words with leaves upon a tree. Horace called upon poets to use only living words. Unlike Horace, however, and much more like the modernists who preceded him, Queneau often appeared to want to make all words live, words spoken in the past as well as those men speak today. Queneau's defense of civilization entails rescuing words from the *alphadécédets*— a newly born word that Queneau coined to designate as cemeteries ("La chair chaude des mots," 193).

Within this neoclassical context Queneau's campaign for "neo-French" makes more sense, for an organic view of language underlies his somewhat quixotic polemic in favor of replacing standard written French with a language that in spelling and syntax would be closer to the speech of ordinary people. The philosophical import of Queneau's polemic is that language must, for the sake of culture's healthy development, be constantly growing and updated. One may well take one's distance vis-à-vis this organic metaphor, and still accept the necessity of attending to language's development; and with this, accept that the function of poets is, as Ezra Pound put it, to "keep language efficient."[10] Nothing might be more efficient, in Queneau's view, than a language that no longer convinced us of our fallen state.

Queneau's poetic practice is a coherent attempt, then, to renew language and render it innocent through an exploitation of the festive impulse and its often transgressive parody. Not the least of his goals is to oblige us to evaluate critically the codified uses of language that tradition has bequeathed us, for lucidity is the goal of poetry as well as science. But a good many of the stylistic inventions

Queneau uses for his transgression have little to do with popular or oral language; his arsenal of transgressive weapons includes neologisms, puns, scientific and foreign words, archaic terms, and arbitrary spellings, as well as comic transpositions of popular usage. In this poetry frequently about poetry Queneau often enacts a verbal comedy about the possibilities of poetry that aims ultimately at renewing the tradition. This self-reflexivity is not mere narcissism, but part of the Orphic task of keeping language ready for whatever nature—or perhaps even history—might demand of it.

## Chapter Four
# The Novels: The Thirties and the Occupation

Queneau's novels are much like his poems in that they are an attempt to renew narrative forms, often through parody, and to recast the language of literature. His first novel, *The Bark Tree*, contains an extraordinary parody of most of the conventions of realistic fiction. At a time when relativity theory and quantum mechanics had suddenly rendered untenable the Newtonian underpinnings of realism, Queneau seems to have wanted to write in this remarkable first novel a narrative that, with cosmic gusto, would offer an approach to representation that might be consonant with the new physics. Commonsense notions about time, space, and our understanding of the coordinates of identity undergo radical transformation in this novel. *The Bark Tree* also enacts an intellectual comedy that draws upon the Western philosophical tradition and many of the interpretations of reality that this tradition proposes. Part of the book's legend is, as we said earlier, that Queneau set out, in writing *The Bark Tree,* to translate Descartes's *Discourse on Method* into popular French. In a sense Descartes had given an example for this translation, since, by writing in French and not in Latin, Descartes had demonstrated that any language can be a vehicle for the expression of ideas. Queneau's tremendous variety of diction in this novel might well be ascribed to a Cartesian ambition: to make ordinary language capable of expressing ultimate reality, even if, in Queneau's case, that reality is finally dissolved in the play of appearances that delights the festive and skeptical mind.

The central dilemma of the Cartesian philosopher is to distinguish true from deceiving appearances. Queneau forces readers to confront this problem from the novel's outset by obliging them to evaluate appearances that are observed by a surrogate novelist-character from within the book. This observer, Pierre Le Grand, begins the novel by looking at the most banal of Parisian scenes, the rush hour crowds struggling to catch their subway to go home. This observer fixes his attention on an unknown bank employee named Etienne Marcel who, transformed into a Cartesian questioner, later becomes an observer of appearances in his turn. All of Queneau's observers may be likened to Cartesian philosophers looking for certainty; but in the case of Pierre Le Grand, he also resembles Heisenberg's physicist whose observations modify what is observed. Pierre's act of observing Etienne endows this initially one-dimensional character with new dimensions so that Etienne is transformed into that ideal of realist fiction, a "three-dimensional" character. But in the world of relativity physics the fixed observation point of the Cartesian observer is, if not an illusion, merely an arbitrarily chosen point. One can multiply indefinitely the number of observation points for viewing the "real," and so Queneau offers the reader an "I" who observes Pierre, as well as other characters who intervene directly to tell what they see. No one, however, can penetrate one of the central mysteries of the book, which is Pierre's appearance: is he a character, a magician, or perhaps a gangster with a "Cantorian" brother? (And the allusion to set theory might suggest a mathematical model for describing observers observing observers.)

With a cast of characters who sometimes have more than one identity, Queneau offers a disjointed narration that is as much a parody of the realist concept of plot as a device of stringing together experiments in narrative modes and diction. Narrative lines crisscross and set up situations in which the characters are puzzled and taken in by the appearances of events and other characters. Coincidences abound, but to a purpose: Queneau's use of surprising coincidences embodies another form of self-reflexivity by which the novel demonstrates its consciousness of itself as a game construct. (For those who believe numbers provide motivation, there is also a fairly elaborate numerological system underlying much of the plot.)[1]

Observing Etienne, Pierre follows him to his suburban home where this nobody lives with his son and attractive wife. She in turn is observed and followed by the womanizing Narcense and Potice. The latter is "laminated" by a bus, which is in turn observed by a Madame Cloche whose brother Dominique owns the "dive" in which Pierre and Etienne eventually meet. Narcense, moreover, lives in a building where he is observed by the would-be writer and concierge Saturnin, none other than the brother of Madame Cloche. They all join in observing the old man Taupe—literally "father mole"—an impoverished junk dealer who has placed a blue door against the railway embankment that serves as a wall to his hovel. When Madame Cloche decides that Taupe must have a treasure hidden behind the door, she reasons from appearances to decide that Pierre and Etienne must be gangsters who wish to seize the treasure. Desirous of seizing it herself, she arranges a marriage of Taupe with the servant girl Ernestine—which allows Queneau to narrate an extraordinary marriage "banquet" that owes as much to Socrates and *The Phaedo* as to Flaubert's wedding scene in *Madame Bovary*. All pursue the nonexistent treasure, but Taupe dies and, coincidentally, war breaks out between the French and the Etruscans. In the meantime, the parasitic dwarf Bébé Toutout (another doggy figure) has forced himself on Etienne's household as an uninvited guest.

The novel takes on a flagrantly absurdist character, even if prophetic of history to come. Etienne is mobilized to fight the "macaroni eaters," Dominique sets up a brothel in Epinal, Etienne's wife, Alberte (Queneau's homage to Proust's Albertine), leaves with Narcense, and finally Etienne's son Theo (God?) and the diabolical Bébé Toutout set up their own whorehouse. In a final flaunting of its self-reflexivity the novel ends "decades later" in a confrontation between Etienne and Miss Aulini—or Madame Cloche sounding like Mussolini. Tired of the way the novel has been observing them, the characters decide to *littératurer* ("literase") the entire book and to return to the beginning. A "mask" flies through the air, a narrator-"persona," in that word's original sense of mask, obliterating time and bringing back the novel's opening lines. The completed circle is—as Parmenides held in his *Way of Truth*—the only figure that can describe the nature of what is. Time is abolished for these characters, much as it is for those elusive particles that quantum mechanics offers as the building blocks of the universe. Queneau undoubtedly anticipates the "Tao of physics" by several decades, not to mention *Finnegans Wake*.

*The Bark Tree* preceded *Finnegans Wake,* but it appeared several years after Joyce's *Ulysses,* and Queneau's most obvious homage to that seminal novel is the way he uses different narrative modes throughout the novel. Queneau eschews Joyce's systematic exploitation of a different narrative mode for each chapter. In good Rabelaisian fashion he seems to delight in breaks in tonality and style by leaping from one mode to another: narration by letters, dialogues and conversations, first-person soliloquies, telegrams, catalogs, Flaubertian indirect discourse, interior monologue or stream of consciousness, dream hallucinations, mock heroic discourse, newspaper articles, and narration from a dog's point of view, to name a few of the fifteen or twenty modes Queneau playfully adopts. Each narrative mode offers a different point of view for seizing the "real," though the proliferation of these points of view finally burlesques the idea of a seizure of whatever one might be tempted to call reality. As we said, the world has as many possible appearances as there are possible observation points, and these can be multipled by the number of means of transcribing, in an indefinite number of modes, those appearances. In this sense Queneau goes beyond Joyce in smashing the Newtonian coordinates of realist fiction, for the Irish novelist had kept his world limited to a fairly fixed time and place.

Queneau seems to have been partially in Joyce's thrall in his creation of characters. In *Ulysses* Joyce's characters act out their daily life on a historical day in modern Dublin, but they are also reflections of mythic counterparts from the *Odyssey*. In his creation of characters Queneau uses the history of Western thought much as Joyce used myth: nearly every character in *The Bark Tree* embodies, to a greater or lesser degree, a historical thinker, such as Parmenides, Socrates, Descartes, and Hegel. At the same time his characters, like Joyce's, are set in the most banal and fallen reality—or appearances—of the modern city. Much of Queneau's comedy depends on the misfit existing between the historical world of ideas and the everyday world of Paris, though it is the reader's task to perceive this misfit. No more than Joyce's Bloom in *Ulysses* is conscious of being Odysseus are Queneau's characters aware that they speak with the voices of philosophers. (None of them could ever be accused of reading anything more bookish than a newspaper.) They speak their thoughts, and in Queneau's transposition of popular language one finds echoes of those philosophical solutions that Queneau, if not Etienne Marcel or Madame Cloche, sees as the recurring archetypes of Western thought.

Old man Taupe, for example, that most miserable of bums, has hit upon his own version of Epicurean thought, with its stoic defense mechanisms. Having reached total ruin, he has found happiness, for no further disaster can menace him. Having found the freedom from fear that Epicurus recommended as the goal of all activity, he can content himself with the simple pleasures that constitute Epicurean moderation. Queneau enacts a good-humored parody of the limits of Epicurean thought when the old bum is tempted by Ernestine's thighs. Epicurus discouraged marriage, and Taupe's aspiration to sensual bliss brings about his demise when he allows himself to fall into the clutches of Madame Cloche, Narcense, and Saturnin—those deluded conspirators who, like Epicurus, think that appearances might be reality.

Much of *The Bark Tree* turns on the central Platonic and Cartesian question about what is real beyond appearances. At the novel's outset Theo, Etienne's son, is shown reading an *Apology of Socrates,* but his eyes have circles less from meditating on Platonic ideas than from contemplating an obscene photo he has hidden in the volume. Appearances are deceptive. Queneau's slapstick use of Plato reaches its high point when Ernestine, suddenly dying after her wedding banquet, assumes the "pose of Socrates drinking hemlock" and proceeds to deliver a final discourse that, in Parisian slang, reasons out the nonexistence of the soul. Her anticlerical conclusions are quite the opposite of those Socrates reached; but Queneau's Platonism has always contained a parodistic anti-Platonism in it, exemplary of which is Narcense's discovery early in the book that the essence of things is to have no essence. Transitory appearances are often as disgustingly real as they appear to be.

Saturnin, the concierge who tries to write, may well be a reflection of Saturninus, a Gnostic heretic who believed the world was a disgustingly fallen place. He also believed that since the world was created by an evil creator, nothing could be known about the true god of light. As for Queneau's Saturnin, he wants to be a creator himself, though in his attempt to write he discovers that he is not thinking his own langauge. On the contrary, language flows through his head, and he has little power over it. This discovery that language may be thinking him, rather than the contrary, leads him to suspect that what he really has in his head is—nothing. At this point Saturnin may appear to be inhabited by a gnostic deity; or perhaps a negative theologian or an existentialist who, like the Heidegger of *What is Metaphysics,* paradoxically discovers that nothingness discloses being. It would not be the least of Queneau's jokes to make of Heidegger a contemporary version of a Gnostic.

Saturnin later echoes Parmenides and Plato in one of the high points of early pataphysical logic in Queneau. He discovers that he can write about what does not exist; hence he can entertain as an object of thought that nothingness that Plato, after Parmenides,

said could not be thought. Playing with the parodoxes Plato confronted in *Parmenides* and *The Sophist,* Queneau also makes of Saturnin
a Hegelian who finds that the truth encompasses the totality of
what is as well as what is not. For it is as important a truth about
a "pat of butter" to say that it is not on the table as to say that it
*is* on the table. Of course there are an infinite number of things
that aren't, and in their nonbeing they acquire a curious sort of
being that delights the novelist—who writes about what is not—
if it dismays the philosopher. Willed confusions about being and
nonbeing are after all the stuff of fictions. Moreover, Queneau's
mixing ideas taken from Parmenides, Plato, and Hegel is a way of
dismantling any monist thought that would reduce the world and
its reality to a single principle, be it Parmenides' "the One" or
Hegel's absolute spirit. Queneau, the novelist, has his first loyalty
to the heterogeneous and the disparate, and his parodistic celebration
of the incongruous is a declaration of his refusal of reductive thought—
of which Parmenides' claim that there is only the One is the most
wonderful perduring example.

If there are a central character and a central theme to *The Bark
Tree,* they are to be found in Etienne and his Cartesian quest for a
principle of certain knowledge. Like Descartes, he has his moment
of hyperbolic doubt when he doubts everything. Facing Taupe's
enigmatic door he wonders if everything he perceives has just begun
to exist (a possibility that Descartes allowed with his supposition
that an evil spirit might constantly deceive him). Doubting appearances has, however, its limitations, as Etienne notes when he
reflects on Madame Cloche's belief that he is a gangster. She has
obviously doubted Etienne's appearing to be what he thinks he is,
an honest, scrupulous, married bank employee; she has gone on to
discover Etienne's "real being." Therefore, Etienne reasons, he must
somehow have the appearances of a gangster. And with this paradox,
Cartesian reasoning seems to disintegrate in the very impossibility
of deciding what an appearance might be. Perhaps it is hardly
surprising that, confronting Madame Cloche at the end of the novel,
Etienne prefers to erase the whole thing.

With regard to its setting, *The Bark Tree* anchors Etienne's world
of appearances in a marginal world that represents metonymically
the fallen average everydayness one finds in Queneau's poetry. In
Paris and the suburbs "black masses" of human beings wait for
trains on platforms that recall "flypaper."[2] It is a world where

nondescript rooms, rotting slowly away, await the voyager to the suburbs who, like Pierre Le Grand, is obliged to spend a night there: "he remembered with horror the night he had spent at Hippolyte's; the sheets so filthy that he had preferred to sleep fully dressed, the smell of mildew that came from a bedside table of a most uncommon style; the layer of thick dust floating on the water intended for his washstand; the sickly, yellowish light that had pretensions to illuminating the whole, and, above all, the feeling of abandonment he had experienced . . ." (30). In a sense urban civilization is abandonment, abandonment to all the ugliness, pollution, and general dreck that proliferate around the capital. Suffering, like Flaubert, from the temptation to exorcise human stupidity, in *The Bark Tree* Queneau often attempts to see how far he can go in exploring the absurd fall into being's degradation. His comedy turns less on a despair about finding "reality" than on a disabused contempt for a reality that is not perhaps worth finding in the first place.

Queneau's secular Jansenism notwithstanding, *The Bark Tree* is one of the most truly innovative novels in the twentieth century. Proposing narrative structures that integrate a relativist sense of frameworks of understanding, the novel enacts a great comedy of the literary, philosophical, and scientific systems that allow (or do not allow) men to make sense of their existence. The disparities between these systems and the fallen world, often measured by the incongruously popular language that Queneau uses to give voice to these systems, creates an original novelistic vision that, among other things, clearly marked the end of the realist hegemony that from Balzac through Jules Romain has dominated French fiction.

After *The Bark Tree* Queneau published a second novel, *Gueule de Pierre* (Face of stone, 1934). Since this novel, along with *Les Temps mêlés* (Uncertain weather, 1941), is now incorporated into a later novel, Queneau's *Saint Glinglin* (1948), I will consider these novels as a single work in the following chapter. The next work that concerns us is Queneau's third novel, *Les Derniers Jours* (The last days), published in 1938. This novel has certain autobiographical affinities with the preceding *Gueule de pierre* in that both present the tribulations of a student who is modeled on Queneau and his student days. Both works present wry distillations of the grandeur and folly of student attempts to master the world. In *Les Derniers Jours*, Queneau has incorporated clearly autobiographical elements into a broad intellectual comedy that also shares certain traits of *The Bark Tree*. He sets forth a series of characters who circulate, like planets in a solar system, about the fixed center of a Parisian café, revolving about an ever-present waiter named Alfred.

This astronomical metaphor presents both a description of the novel's structure and an emblem of the comedy of representation enacted therein. At the fixed center of this universe is Alfred, the waiter who is disdainful of a "certain Einstein" who is frequently in the news. For Alfred has no trouble interpreting the universe from his fixed viewpoint by reading the stars, or magnetic forces, and especially by figuring gambling odds. Einstein's relativity theory is of little use to this waiter who, using popular means of understanding, can combine probabilities to figure out with complete accuracy which horses are going to win the races, and thus recoup a fortune his father once lost gambling.

Queneau's comedy has a double edge. On the one hand, the burlesque image of a Copernican solar system describes the way his characters cyclically fulfill their banal destinies: studies, sexual initiation, growing old, and dying. Alfred's periodic commentaries on the characters expresses Queneau's amused distance vis-à-vis the essential banality of existence. On the other hand, post-Copernican science offers representation of the universe that hardly seem banal, but which also seem of little use for making sense of our daily experience. What can it mean to a café waiter that, as Einstein claimed, a moving clock marks time more slowly than a clock at rest? How can one win at the races with that knowledge? The gap between relativity theory and life in *Les Derniers Jours* is as great as is the disparity in *The Bark Tree* between the suburban dive and Saturnin's Hegelian-Platonic speculations on being and nonbeing.

Alfred, the "philosopher" café waiter, is metaphorically the fixed point around which circle a series of characters living in the banal universe of fallen existence. Queneau offers interweaving narrative strands that relate, alternately, the first days of students in Paris and the last days of old men living out their life. There are numerous students, though the central character is Vincent Tuquedenne, a student who, like most of the characters, comes from Queneau's Le Havre. Among the older men two characters stand out, Tolut, a retired lycée professor of geography and history, and Brabbant, a petty swindler having several aliases. These two men are nearly paired characters. Their encounter on a Parisian street, when Brabbant tries to swindle Tolut, sets the novel in motion; and it is Tolut's throwing himself from a street curb into the path of an automobile that ends the work with a willed catastrophe. Between these two events we watch the characters come together, separate, and return as they move through the orbit of their destiny.

Brabbant, for example, yearns for a great destiny, but is in reality a petty criminal, with cyclical libidinous urges, who lives on swindling tourists. He plays billiards in the café with Tolut, acquires a young mistress, but can hit upon no great scheme for making money until, by accident, a friend offers to invest money in a fictitious project Brabbant had dreamed up on the spur of the moment. He wants to invest money in real estate in Germany, believing that it will increase in value when the German mark gains in value after the French have occupied the Ruhr Valley (in 1923). This financial analysis is followed, of course, by the greatest period of inflation that Germany ever knew. Yet, ironically, Brabbant dies with all the appearances of an honest and prosperous man, for, as Alfred notes, he ends up with a luxury townhouse and money in the bank.

In Brabbant we might see a portrait of the "practical man" who is deluded by the active life. Contrasting with him is Professor Tolut who, in leading a "contemplative" life, falls prey to quite as many delusions. In his retirement Tolut discovers that he has been a swindler of sorts, since he taught geography without ever having traveled, and therefore he did not really "know" what he taught. In his advancing senility he applies the same reasoning to the teaching of history and concludes, rather madly, that he has been a double swindler. He dreams of traveling in order to assuage some of his guilt feelings, and when his brother dies in London, Tolut makes his first foray out of France. Queneau's amused disdain for travel is reflected in Tolut's experience across the channel: he discovers that people speak an incomprehensible Foreign Language, gets lost, receives his brother's final malediction, and forgets to visit the capital's sights. One of Queneau's supreme comic creations, Tolut is a man dementedly torn by the contrast between language and referent, words and things. He ends up a kind of distorted Hamlet figure, first imagining schemes for frustrating death, then searching for Yorick's (and his own) skull before finally embracing his destiny with his suicide.

Contrasting with the old men who grow senile and die are the students who are setting out, nearly all attracted by often dubious schemes for advancement. Queneau's portrayal of youth is most immediately illuminated, not by a comparison with his own student days, but rather by contrasting it with the work of André Gide. Queneau has certainly attempted to bring a corrective to the vision of students that Gide had proposed in such novels as *The Counterfeiters* and *Lafcadio,* the latter being a novel that Vincent reads himself. Gide's young protagonist Lafcadio commits a gratuitous murder to see if his reflexes are still intact. Queneau's Vincent, in pointed contrast, leads a life of quiet boredom in which all manifestations of Gidean energy are conspicuously lacking. His greatest adventure is to have surgery performed on his sinuses.

Vincent comes to Paris to study philosophy. Living at first in a miserable hotel, his life can be reduced to a quick résumé by the list he keeps of his daily expenses for coffee and subway. He wanders in the Parisian streets and thinks alternately about Western culture and nothing, mainly the latter. Vincent is the first representative of what we might call Queneau's prototypical hero, later exemplified by Pierrot and Valentin Brû, a hero whose fundamental trait is to be existentially vacuous. However, a great deal of intellectual energy is generated by this emptiness, and Vincent seems to be attracted by every literary and philosophical movement that could interest a young student or writer in those experimental years of the early twenties. Interested in dada, reading Proust and Gide, concocting a philosophical system that proves that the Parmenidean "One" must be, Vincent also has his Thomistic period, discovers Apollinaire, Max Jacob, and cubism, and, coincidentally, loses his virginity. But, mainly, he lives his boredom, knowing he knows nothing.

In his portrayal of Vincent and the various students with whom he associates, Queneau presents both the cycle of initiation that characterizes youth and a somewhat satirical version of Paris's creative effervescence immediately after World War I. Vincent's friends serve to round out this portrayal. One friend, Hublin, is interested in spiritualism, but commits a gratuitous Gidean crime that forces him to leave the country. Another friend, Rohel, spends most of his time chasing women; but even he is sufficiently interested in current happenings to steal a recent translation of Freud. Other students are content to learn what they are told to learn, since in any case they would prefer drinking and carousing. The cycle of initiation varies little.

In terms of structure *Les Derniers Jours* is unique in Queneau's work. In this novel Queneau made his one effort at the modernist attempt to spatialize form. By spatialization of form we mean that, in breaking the various narrative lines into intersecting patches of narration, Queneau constructs a work that suggests the simultaneity of presence of all the parts. The effect is like the simultaneous presence of all the revolving parts of a textual mobile. Queneau is of course too ironically disengaged from his work to offer it, in the manner of other experimental writers, as a means for overcoming the metaphysical linearity of time or writing. Nor does this work purport to show that form is a means of discovery. The comic self-consciousness with which the novel orchestrates these crossing narrative orbits, especially as exemplified by Alfred's remarks on the cyclical behavior of everyone, shows that for all its modernist guise the novel is a kind of antimodernist demonstration: new literary forms do little more than reveal the dreary if comic sameness of destinies that could be represented in at least ninety-nine other ways. Queneau was a neoclassical writer even when experimenting with modernist exercises in style.

The autobiographical side of *Les Derniers Jours* is subordinated to Queneau's creation of a narrative mobile. In his fourth novel, however, autobiography breaks through the fictional surfaces to such an extent that Queneau, undoubtedly motivated by excessive modesty, did not wish to have the book republished. *Odile* (1937) is a roman à clef, and the reader inevitably takes pleasure in identifying historical figures from the surrealist period, such as André Breton or Louis Aragon, who figure in this rather ferocious attack on surrealism and its pretensions. In literary terms, too, the novel is singular in Queneau's work in that it is a first-person narrative, a nearly classical *récit* that relates with great sobriety and restraint the difficulty of growing up.

Though using different characters and narrative conventions, *Odile* continues the description of the education that Vincent had begun in *Les Derniers Jours*. *Odile's* narrator, Bernard Travy, begins his tale where Vincent's ended, with the period of obligatory military service. More precisely, Travy's tale begins with his "birth" on a road in Morocco, some time in the early twenties, when he sees, in a passing Arab, a figure who resembles at once a noble man, a poet, and a philosopher. From this point on his memory of his childhood is obliterated, and his first twenty-one years of life disappear as into a period of prenatal existence. *Odile* is more or less contemporary with *Chêne et chien,* Queneau's "novel in verse," and it seems clear that the novel begins with the same refusal of childhood experience and its unhappiness that the poem exorcises. Projecting his desire for nobility upon the Arab, Travy refuses his childhood through a willed repression of the past. This refusal of childhood is also complementary to that moment in the novel when Travy decides to break with the poet Anglarès and his followers, those revolutionaries modeled on the surrealists, who have proclaimed the supposedly magical period of childhood to be an ideal state. Travy finds they are playing at being children because they are incapable of any other activity.

The novel concludes with Travy's decision to accept the love of a woman, Odile, and to live with her as man and wife. The itinerary that leads from the opening refusal through his rupture with surrealism takes Bernard through a time of experimentation in which he learns that he cannot be content with a marginal existence while he plays at being a psychic revolutionary. Returning to Paris after his military service he fills his days by devoting himself to mathematics, covering countless pages with endless equations. He also begins to frequent a group of *affranchis*—a group of pimps and their women. In this milieu he meets Odile, another bourgeois rebel who has chosen to break with her background as best she can.

Contrasting with the *affranchis* are the poets and artists who gather around Anglarès. This fictional poet, like his real model, is quite disdainful of science and mathematics. He is, however, willing to find in Travy's explanations of mathematics another proof that the world of rationality is collapsing before the onslaught of the unconscious mind. Since Bernard's description of mathematics is a fairly straightforward Platonist view of mathematical reality, it is clear that Anglarès hears only what he wishes to hear. In any case, Bernard is admitted to the group, though he is never overly enthusiastic about the group's desire to transform the nature of consciousness, especially since it is evident that Anglarès's main goal is really to frequent the world of upper-class countesses.

The latter part of the novel centers on Travy's revolt against middle-class conventions, especially such banalities as love and marriage. He refuses quite simply to recognize that Odile has become essential to him. To enable Odile to return to Paris after she has no other resources, Bernard decides to marry her, but *not* to live with her, so that she can lead her own life. With a pittance that an eccentric uncle provides, he sets her up in a hotel room, only to lead a miserable existence as he strives to keep her at a distance, even rebuffing her so as not to appear a victim of his own conventional impulses. It is in Greece that Bernard's recognition of his need for this woman comes to him like an epiphany, at the same time he admires the work of a Greek fisherman and he suddenly rediscovers what he calls the lost meaning of numbers. In Greece he comes to grips with his shame about being ordinary and learns to accept the "human simplicity" that will allow him to live. His period of ascesis is over, and in a very real sense he has come to a wisdom that allows him to embrace the world.

*Odile* is, then, a love story of sorts, and a successful one at that. It affirms, moreover, the necessity of accepting the banality of what is. Yet, the novel is no apology of facility, nor does it offer the banal as an ideal. Bernard achieves happiness here as the result of an ascetic reduction that reveals the primordial simplicity of what a man can reasonably expect only after trials and despair. *Odile* makes explicit what is often only implicit in Queneau's other novels and their comic celebration of the trivial: the comic can be a form of ascetic reduction that forces one to see how few and ordinary are the truths one can encompass. In a moving letter to Queneau, Max Jacob compared *Odile* to a work that might have been written by Dostoyevski, but without the Russian's romanticism.[3] There is indeed an antiromanticism in Travy's refusal of love, for he refuses, with scorn, to live life as if it were the subject of a novel. But Queneau's negative version of a Madame Bovary also finds that his life is a novel, the powerful novel that is written to record his victory over himself. *Odile* proposes a redemption that is a secular equivalent to the salvation that Dostoyevski often grants his characters.

The redemption motif surfaces again in Queneau's next novel, *Les Enfants du Limon* (The children of mire), published in 1938. Central to Queneau's cosmology in this novel is a genealogy in which all the characters descend, in various ways, from a common father, now dead, but who might be likened to a god or demiurge who created them all from mud. Salvation is again a central issue in the fallen world, though Queneau's characters must seek their redemption in the historical world of twentieth-century political and economic upheavals. There is here an almost bitter portrayal of the social world; and Queneau is vehement in his denunciation of the wealthy. Queneau is not Louis Aragon, however, and the novel is not a work of socialist realism. The portrayal of the social reality of the thirties is doubled by a long series of demented representations of the world that Queneau took from his research on literary madmen. Queneau attributes his own research to one of his characters who can in turn read and quote long excerpts from it. These quotations often double the action taking place in the historical world of the novel. The delirious ravings of the mad and the representation of French society in the thirties complement each other like Gnostic mirror images.

Queneau's social comedy is enacted by a series of characters who are nearly all relatives of Jules Limon, an industrialist who commits suicide after the beginning of the world depression. Although their fortune is in danger, the grandchildren of Limon—Agnès, Noémie, and Daniel—lead the decadent life of the idle rich, with vacations in southern France where they give themselves over to sports and tourism. Here they are admired by lower-class characters to whom, it turns out, they are related. The Italian grocer Gramigni ("Weeds" or *chiendent*) marries a Limon maid named Clémence, who is Limon's illegitimate daughter. Another lower-class character, named Bossu, is in reality the illegitimate son of the lycée supervisor Chambernac, himself the brother-in-law of Sophie, Limon's daughter. Class differences notwithstanding, it would appear that we are all children of mire, or perhaps brothers and sisters in the muck.

Within this nearly allegorical framework Queneau narrates a series of events that are dependent upon their reference to history for their full significance. For example, Gramigni is in France because fascism has forced him into exile even as it has killed two of his brothers. The fate of the Limon family is directly tied to history, since, with the stock market crash, Sophie's second husband, Baron Hachamoth, must try to keep the family solvent by selling the villa in the south and reducing family expenditures. The family continues to live in the fashionable Parisian suburb of Neuilly, and the latter part of the novel takes place in Paris, during the political turmoil of 1934, when France was shaken by a nearly successful right-wing coup.

Politics directly enters the novel when Agnès and her husband found a protofascist organization called the "Nation without Classes." Agnès is possessed by an inverted political idealism wherein she becomes convinced that she could be her nation's savior. But her political league rapidly becomes involved in the kind of thug tactics that often characterize the politics of the extreme right in France, and her fate is to be killed in the streets during the attempted coup.

Her brother Daniel also ends up a victim of mania. Suffering asthma attacks, he discovers evil and then a biblical explanation for evil's existence. Queneau seems, in the characters of Agnès and Daniel, to be contrasting the forms of fanaticism that contemporary man has hit upon in his quest for salvation: fascism and religious delusion. But in his depiction of Daniel's suffering Queneau creates one of the most powerful moments in his fiction: Daniel's suffocation becomes his world, and no rationalization can seemingly justify the absolute nature of his suffering.

Yet creation is redeemed in *Les Enfants du Limon.* Noémie, in a case of biblical incest, marries her uncle Astolphe, Sophie's brother. After leading a parasitic life, Astolphe becomes a dealer in rags and old paper, and then a manufacturer of paper. His task is to redeem matter, to transform waste into enduring parchment. Moreover, he and Noémie have a child whose birth marks the end of the novel with the sign of *délivrance,* a biblical term that one might translate as birth, but also as liberation and an implied salvation in the midst of the twentieth century's ongoing history of fanaticisms.

Within this plot—and nearly overpowering it—is intercalated the story of Chambernac's attempt to compile an "Encyclopedia of Inexact Sciences," or an anthology of writings by literary cranks like the one that Queneau himself had compiled at the beginning of the thirties. In a sense Queneau is redeeming his own work by quoting excerpts from this dementia for which he never found a publisher. This documentary side of the novel confronts the reader with a collection of crank writings: claims about squaring the circle, mad cosmologies, and delirious sciences, as well as paranoid versions of French history. These writings are varied representations of the world as cast by the inventive minds of the delirious whose fiction-making capacities often rival those of the best novelists, not to mention scientists and historians. Queneau is fascinated by the multiplicity of heterogeneous orders of representation that the mind can spin forth, even if, as Chambernac observes about this project, there is something equally as demented about the desire to catalog all these ravings. Yet, Hegel's declaration that the real is the rational left him with an impoverished encyclopedia, for the total encyclopedia of the human mind would demand nothing less than a place for every product it has conceived—including vast tomes of delirium.

As Queneau noted about the comparable project that Flaubert undertook in *Bouvard and Pécuchet,* the encyclopedic urge is Faustian. With proper irony Queneau therefore gives Chambernac a Faustian helper, a poor devil named Purpulan (who learned his trade from Bébé Toutout). He signs a pact to help Chambernac for four years, and the two begin classifying a library that Chambernac had inherited—inheritance being the glue that seemingly ties the world and its traditions together. Chambernac's cataloging project immediately brings up the question of the criteria by which one can differentiate the ravings of the mad or of cranks from the normal erroneous or visionary writings that our culture accords an honorable place in its anthologies of inherited writings. What differentiates, say, the biblical version of creation from the cosmology of August B——, whose anonymous brochure proposed cold as the primordial cosmic force that, in producing ice that melted, gave rise to the mud *(limon)* that now constitutes the interior shores of immensity? One suspects that Queneau believed that it is often only the arbitrary acceptance by the collective community that differentiates myth from madness.

Chambernac recognizes that mere anthologizing is hackwork and desires the glory that might come from organizing madness encyclopedically as knowledge. Knowledge demands rational categories, and Chambernac hits upon a four-part schema: the Circle, the World, the Word, and Time. Time, for example, would include the counterhistories of France as told by those cranks who dispute the received versions of historical reality. It would appear, however, that there are as many versions of history as there are minds that have become unhinged by history.

Chambernac's encyclopedia thus unravels as quickly as he orders it, for what classificatory system can contain within it the proliferating fictions of the mad? What form of knowledge can find a category for, say, a system of social reform that proposes to institute sacred cannibalism as a solution to the world's hunger problem? Chambernac begins to make exceptions to his ordering system to allow "special chapters" for those cranks whose systems especially fascinate him. It is, of course, the very nature of a demented system of knowledge to be a pataphysical exception, and Chambernac's four-part schema is as arbitrary as the knowledge he tries to order with it. The only order that could work is one like that found in the Chinese encyclopedia that Borges describes: a system with a residual category to cover everything that does not fit into all the other categories. Like Borges, Queneau is fascinated with the way fictions refuse our impulse to order and to simplify. Invented by madmen or by novelists, fictions of all sorts can show how unshapely are the lines of demarcation between the imaginary and knowledge.

There is, however, more to Chambernac's proposed "Encyclopedia of Inexact Sciences" than a demonstration of the demented side of the desire to order all the products of the mind. Nicolas Hewitt has proposed that Queneau intended for motifs and events recorded in the encyclopedia to mirror characters and events in the novel's plot.[4] The ravings of cranks are ironic doubles for the historical world of the novel itself. One must stress that there is nothing systematic in this doubling, but there is a kind of general Mephistophelian irony in the way one can note similarities between the encyclopedia and the events that engulf Astolphe, Agnès, Daniel, and other characters. This irony functions to designate Queneau's own cosmology, portraying in the novel the children of mire, as but another version of the many mad cosmologies that cranks have succeeded in having published (with the added irony that Queneau did not succeed in having his *Fous littéraires* published). There is also an ironic overlap in the way the children are seized by manias and elaborate crank versions of reality. Agnès is, for example, a fascist megalomaniac, who could just as well be a Leninist in her belief that it is her destiny to save France. Never afraid of self-directed irony, Queneau makes of Daniel an asthmatic who, after discovering the existence of evil, first adopts a kind of Gnostic vision of creation and then, having read the Bible, decides that the "rivers of Hell have overrun their banks" (219). The bastard Bossu represents lower-class paranoia in that he comes to believe that cosmic powers have somehow conspired against him, the embodiment of "superman"; his decision to become a police informer doubles the encyclopedia's chapter on French history as told by police informers. Or, as we have noted, Chambernac's very effort to order an encyclopedia mirrors the effort of the mad to create new cosmological orders, a state of affairs Chambernac recognizes when he meditates on the fact that his own project entitles him to be called a "literary crank."

This irony appropriates the entire novel as another instance of literary madness, for we know that it is Queneau who wrote the novel and had the project of compiling an "Encyclopedia of Inexact

Sciences." This ironic turn is completed when Queneau, in one of his most successful examples of ironic self-reflexivity, steps into the novel as a character himself. Having found no publisher for his useless encyclopedia, Chambernac runs into a certain Raymond Queneau whom he had already met in several publishers' offices. Chambernac gives the encyclopedia to this Queneau, who wants to use it in a novel of his in which a character is writing just such an encyclopedia. Queneau is even willing to put Chambernac's name on the cover of the novel, since there figures in the book a character who, like Chambernac, is the headmaster of a lycée and who one day meets a devil. Like Astolphe, who redeems matter by transforming old paper, Queneau has redeemed his old papers by transforming them into a novel, or at least integrating them into a work that embodies the fictions of real madness within a real fiction that is a successful novel. Novelists and rag dealers—both occupations that deal with fallen matter in the real and not too unreal world—are joined in a common project of minimalist salvation.

Queneau is rarely thought of as a political novelist, but the negative portrayal of high society in *Les Enfants du Limon* has clear ideological implications. Perhaps even more explicitly political is *Un Rude Hiver (A Hard Winter),* which appeared in 1939, on the eve of war with Hitler's Germany. The "hard winter" in question is not, however, a contemporary season, but rather one set in 1916, during the long winter of World War I when the war had stalled in the endless bog of trench warfare. This novel is, however, as much a parable for the late thirties as it is a representation of the viewpoint of Queneau's singular hero, a pro-German Frenchman in 1916. Few such Frenchmen existed in 1916, but there were a good many Frenchmen in 1939 who preferred Hitler to the recent Jewish Prime Minister Léon Blum. The reader should keep in mind this double historical perspective when reading *A Hard Winter,* for the novel offers the portrayal of a kind of reactionary mind that Queneau may have first encountered in his father, but which threatened to turn France over to the Nazis when Queneau was writing his novel.

Queneau's hero is a right-wing Hamlet, Bernard Lehameau (whose name means "the hamlet" in French). He is a thirty-three-year-old lieutenant who, wounded in Charleroi in 1914, is convalescing in his native Le Havre. Having lost his wife thirteen years before, he is a widower who has long had no contact with women. It is hardly surprising that he should meet and court an English WAAC, Miss

Weeds, but it is a bit more perplexing that he should also begin frequenting a fourteen-year-old named Annette, the ward of an older sister who is a prostitute. It is finally quite surprising that, in spite of his pro-German sympathies, he should give to a German spy information that allows the Germans to torpedo the hospital ship on which Miss Weeds is sailing to England. Redemption and trans-figuration await this Hamlet, however, first in the form of a sexual encounter with the prostitute sister, and then in the promised nup-tials to a Miss Rousseau—who appears to be the quickly maturing Annette. Sexual redemption powerfully transfigures Bernard, for he finally leaves for the front, no longer hating the poor, in a new state of equilibrium for which eros is more than a little responsible.

Queneau is playing with possible relationships between sexual frustration, pathological behavior, and political attitudes. Bernard's attitudes represent a compendium of protofascist and right-wing political views: he is pro-German, fears "the yellow peril," and hates those workers who can afford to eat decently. Secretly yearning for a strong German leader who can rid Europe of communists, Jews, and Freemasons, he detests all the groups that support the French Republic. Bernard is nearly demented, a point Queneau underscores by borrowing from Céline's recent virulent anti-Semitic polemic of the late thirties when Bernard claims that one need only look at the noses of the Bourbon kings to see that they, too, were Jewish.

After letting the woman he supposedly loves go down on a tor-pedoed boat, this Hamlet denounces the German spy, Frédéric, to whom he had given the information, primarily because Frédéric had somehow sullied Bernard's memories of his wife. Frédéric has the bad fortune to be the first in thirteen years to sit at her place in Bernard's dining room. We are perhaps closer to the kinds of path-ologies that Alfred Hitchcock portrays than those of Shakespeare, a pathology of which the sexual roots are implicit but clear. "Sick with desire," Bernard has Miss Weeds destroyed rather than see her leave. Queneau never offers explicit analysis of motivations, but the reader may feel that Bernard destroys Helen in a kind of symbolic reduplication of the death his first wife knew in a cinema fire. This Hamlet takes pleasure in suffering. Like the ascetic Tertullian, who foresaw that the greatest pleasure for the elect in heaven would consist in watching the torments of the damned, he is as much elated by the misery of the downtrodden as by the prospect of twelve bullet holes in Frédéric's skin. Queneau's feat is to elicit sympathy for Bernard, a monster, but also a victim of the fate that deprived him of a wife or even of the decision of the British authorities to send Miss Weeds away.

Our reference to Hitchcock is appropriate in more than one respect. Cinema relates Bernard's passion for the child-woman Annette to his wife; and going to the movies provides Bernard with an innocent excuse for excursions with Annette and her little brother. Cinema is a leitmotiv in Queneau's work, and it often appears as a festive emblem of popular culture, the nonreflexive culture of the masses that Bernard professes to despise. Bernard finds redemption in Annette, but, one might say, he finds it first at the movies, in their common response to the carnivalesque atmosphere that movies create for the crowds. Queneau's descriptions of the riotous crowds at the cinema depict the suspension of everyday pathologies as people gather to celebrate our popular myths, in westerns and comedies. French children at the movies may boo a documentary on Oxford professors—since they think the robed dignitaries are priests—but they are never mistaken about the subversive joy that animates a film by Charlie Chaplin.

Queneau uses secondary characters in *A Hard Winter* to point up a satire of attitudes toward war. Bernard's brother, a Senator, lives in splendid comfort, far from the front, but never hesitates to indulge himself in mindless jingoism about the ease with which the French will soon know victory over the Germans. Bernard's cousin Lalie has married a Swiss citizen who, in making a fortune in war trafficking, has naturally become a more ardent French patriot than any Frenchman. In contrast to their homicidal patriotism stands Charles, Bernard's nephew, who has actually fought the Germans and knows that they are good soldiers and an adversary worthy of respect. Finally, completing this overview of attitudes is Madame Dutertre, a used-book dealer who once held progressive attitudes and now spends her time speaking diatribes against the congenital stupidity of her fellow citizens. She also reads works of history in which she learns, for example, that at the time of Charles VI and Charles VII war and famine had so reduced the countryside that wolves entered the villages to dig up the corpses of the dead. Such discoveries lead her to reflect, like Queneau of *Une Histoire modèle,* that history is not very funny—a foreshadowing of Queneau's thesis that history can only be the record of human unhappiness.

To conclude our considerations of this deceptively dense novel, we must ask why Queneau has established an intertextual relation with Shakespeare by naming his character "the hamlet." Hamlet appears throughout Queneau's work, and one might see in this vacillating prince a kind of parodistic alter ego for Queneau himself. But parody does not seem to be the issue in *A Hard Winter*. When Bernard goes to the cemetery to meditate on his wife's tomb, two gravediggers show him the skull of the famous singer Ducouillon (roughly "dumb ass") and ask if Bernard had ever heard him at the Opéra Comique. Bernard replies negatively, thus putting an end to the scene and, rather comically, to our expectations that there should follow a parallel with Hamlet's meditation on Yorick. Perhaps Bernard is a negative Hamlet, not feigning madness, but really quite alienated in his mad reactionary ideology. Like Hamlet, he destroys the woman he loves, but apparently with a conscious forethought that hardly characterizes the Danish prince. He is living in a kingdom in which something is truly rotten, but his vision of restoring justice is demented. Again like Hamlet, Bernard is obsessed, a prisoner to a ghost from the past, and in a sense it is this ghost—his wife—that causes him to send the spy Frédéric to the firing squad. As in Shakespeare's play, just retribution can spring from unjust motives and homicidal desires.

Perhaps this play of analogies and counteranalogies is best illuminted by saying that Queneau is writing psychological fiction in which he refuses to engage in psychological analysis. Like many later novelists, Queneau is suspicious that psychological analysis can do little more than explain the known with the unknown, or illuminate the obvious surface with an appeal to dark depths. Queneau's letters to his friend Georges Bataille show that he was interested in studies of sexual psychopathology, but none of this type of analysis figures directly in the novel.[5] Rather, in presenting his character and related events, Queneau contents himself with suggesting analogies with that greater exemplar of feigned and not-so-feigned madness, Hamlet, and allows his readers to interpret this pathological case as they will, at least until Bernard finds his *délivrance* in the redemption that a woman brings him. At this point, as Madame Dutertre observes, he has become a sage.

The question of depths surfaces again, as it were, in Queneau's next novel, *Pierrot mon ami* (My friend Pierrot—translated as *Pierrot*), published during the Occupation in 1942. The novel opens with a certain Tortose telling Pierrot to take off his glasses if he wants to see, and not too surprisingly most of what Pierrot can see is a fog. The novel comes to a close, in the work's epilogue, with Pierrot's imagining what kind of a novel the events in the preceding episodes might have made if one were able to find a pattern for them beneath surface appearances. He "sees" how they could be tied together as an adventure story and that they could have developed as a mystery that might then have resolved itself "like an algebra problem."[6] He "sees" what a detective story the episodes could have made—but did not—complete with a crime, a guilty party, and a detective. Unfortunately he cannot see in them whether or not there really was a central mystery; nor, for that matter, can the reader see any depths beneath the surfaces. We all know that for their proper resolution well-constructed fictions, such as detective stories or tragedies, demand the right glasses for good focus—but the glasses are missing in *Pierrot*.

Pierrot's adventures tease the reader with the "charm of the game of identifications" (153) that consists in seeing things clearly. But *Pierrot* is also a delightfully whimsical tale of a young man, seeking employment on the fringes of society, in the carnival atmosphere of the amusement park. He gets his first job at the fun house, where "philosophers" pay to be situated for a view of girls' panties. He promptly loses it during a brawl. He meets the manager's daughter, Yvonne, a vivacious flirt, but has as little success with her as his clown name, Pierrot, suggests he would. Cupid is the driving force in everyone's life, however, as Pierrot sees when he encounters the manager Pradonnet, his mistress, Léonie, and a recently hired "fakir" named Crouïa-Bey. Léonie has had a good many affairs, and in the fakir she thinks she recognizes her first lover, Jojo Mouilleminche. The fakir says he is Jojo's brother and claims that her lover died after a romantic tryst, years ago in a town named Palinsac, having fallen from a wall surrounding the girl's house.

Details for a possible plot proliferate when Pierrot meets Mounne-zergues, the guardian of a chapel that is somehow situated within the confines of the amusement park. In a flashback that borrows conventions from Gothic novels, mystery movies, and edifying tales, the guardian tells Pierrot how he came to be trusted with the chapel when the Poldevian prince Luigi Voudzoï died after leaping over a wall surrounding the property and falling from his horse. Faithful to his absurd mission the guardian has become an obstacle to the park's enlargement.

Other potential mysteries also unveil themselves. After another brawl at the fun house, Pierrot's friend Petit Pouce is left without a job, but Léonie hires him as a detective and sends him to Palinsac to discover the circumstances in which her lover Jojo might have died. Further matters for elucidation are offered when the amusement park burns down. Suspects are not lacking, nor are versions of how the fire started. Pradonnet is undaunted by the fire's mysterious origins and plans to rebuild on a bigger scale—though one might suspect that the owner of the park, Léonie, is tiring of her lover-manager. At the same time, Pierrot is offered a job by the animal trainer Psermis: he is to take a load of animals to a trainer named Voussois who lives, coincidentally, in Palinsac.

Coincidence is the essence of coherence, and Pierrot's trip south, with his animal friends, abounds in them. It is difficult, however, to say that these coincidences shed much light on anything. He first meets a Heraclitean innkeeper, Posidon, who once had a café near the amusement park. He has never heard of the Poldevian prince's chapel, nor has, at Pierrot's next stop, a hotelkeeper who once was a cashier at the park. He also encounters Léonie and Yvonne, but this coincidence only serves to remind Pierrot how heartbroken he is.

Queneau continues to tease the reader with mysteries by opening the eighth and final chapter with an unnamed character who, on learning from the papers that the amusement park has burned down, observes that it was at the fun house that he learned what Parisian women are about. This unnamed character—he turns out to be Voussois—meets another—Crouïa-Bey—and asks if the tomb in the chapel is still intact. Crouïa-Bey tells that he was recognized in Paris and further relates to Voussois, who is his brother, that he invented a tale for Léonie about Jojo's death. Voussois cannot recall having had a mistress like Léonie, but this is natural; he has had memory problems since his fall from a horse. One may interpret this coincidence as one will, as well as the final series of them. Pierrot arrives, thinks he knows Voussois (because of the prince's portrait in the chapel?); and his arrival is followed by Léonie's and her instantly swooning in Voussois's arms.

The epilogue sheds no more light on these coincidences, even if Pierrot has his one self-reflexive moment when he realizes what a detective story his adventures might have made. There is a resolution of sorts. Léonie and Voussois get rid of Pradonnet, Yvonne marries Pierrot's friend Paradis, and Pierrot misses his chance to become the guardian's adoptive heir when he loses the codicil to Mounnezergues's testament. When Pierrot returns to the old man's house, he finds Yvonne there, obviously the new possessor, though she claims that Mounnezergues is merely away for a while. To which Pierrot's reaction at the end is an outburst of laughter.

Pierrot's laughter is a sign of his acceptance or perhaps even his affirmation that he can confront his past and find that it is truly nothing: no hidden meaning, no depths, no secret pattern. This affirming gesture is what we earlier called Queneau's Nietzschean acceptance of the void through laughter. *Pierrot* is Queneau's most existentialist novel, for it plays with forms that suggest that the past might be endowed with meaning, but which finally point to nothing at all. The past's vacuity is also reflected in the attitudes of other characters, for instance, in the interest that the real Mrs. Pradonnet takes in the story of Léonie and Jojo. She and Léonie were friends at the time of this romance, but she can recall little about it, recognizing that

a past is a funny thing. First of all there are entire parts of it caved in: nothing left. Then there are weeds that have grown up by chance, and you can't recognize anything either. And then there are places that are so pretty that you paint them over every year, first with one color, then with another, and it ends up not looking at all like it once was. Without talking about what one thought was so simple and unmysterious when it happened and that you discover ain't so simple years afterwards. . . . (98)

Her past, like that of Léonie and Pierrot, is like the Poldevian prince: a mystery kept by an obscure chapel whose irritating presence is ignored when it is not contested.

Pierrot appeared shortly after Sartre had given us his existentialist hero in Roquentin and Camus another in Mersault. Pierrot is not so self-reflexive as Sartre's historian who denies the possibility of the past, nor so allegorical as Camus's everyman who proclaims his innocence. Pierrot is the existential clown who thinks mainly about nothing, unless it be the death of Louis XIV, which is rather much the same thing for a young man in need of a job. His alienation, of a rather gentle sort to be sure, consists in his having no control over the events that buffet him about and for which he can find no meaning, no matter how many significant patterns events seem to offer momentarily. He is a pinball-playing hero who is momentarily obliged by the flow of events to be an exegete of his own life, a game for which his prowess with *flippers* has little prepared him. In his notes on the novel, Camus called Pierrot a "lunar creature for whom nothing goes right," equipped with only a "pince-nez, a stock of argot and an unconscious liking for solitary walks."[7]

The existentialist view of the absurd and the genesis of literary meaning dovetail in *Pierrot,* for Queneau obliges the reader as well as Pierrot to question the means they normally employ, in life and in literature, for endowing events with meaning, or for finding significance in recurrent patterns. To those who have a penchant for numerology, for example, Queneau gives eight chapters, eight being the symbol of the infinite. The infinite is a slippery concept, however, and one might well suspect that an infinite number of meanings is equivalent to a null number. At a different level of analysis the recurrence of characters whose names start with *P, M,* and *V* seems to promise some kind of meaningful repetition. The possible identity of Voussois and Prince Voudzoï would even offer the possibility of generating a mystery plot, with consonantal repetitions suggesting the identity of events, such as falling off or over walls. Yet, *Pierrot* never does more than hint that recurrences, such as consonantal repetitions, might have meaning, and the final effect of this game is to demonstrate the arbitrary and often comic choices that go into the construction of literary devices—such as character and plot. With regard to repeating consonants one inevitably thinks of Kafka and his play with the letter *K:* a mere letter suffices to generate a character. In *Pierrot* the repetition of a letter suffices to lay bare the comic interchangeableness of them all.

The play of these repetitions and coincidences is to create another self-reflexive comedy in which the act of reading and its demand for meaning become part of the subject matter. Consonant with the existentialist viewpoint that denies meaning to the world, reading can only turn around a semantic lack residing in the center of the novel and its world. No fullness of completed meaning can ever fill up the lacunae that are generated by unfulfilled suggestions as to where meaning might lie. *Pierrot* is thus the prototype for much later fiction that often takes as its principal theme the quest for meaning produced by the novel's very structure; and it is in this perspective that Queneau can be called the father, if not the big brother, of the French New Novel that flourished in the fifties and sixties. The New Novel, much like *Pierrot* or *The Bark Tree,* often exists as much to demonstrate its own potential functioning as to offer any referential message. This kind of fiction is constructed around a kind of void at its center, a semantic hole that refuses any final meaning as it invites the reader to construct sense anew. Or, as the critic Gaëton Picon observed in distinguishing Queneau from Sartre and Camus, Queneau's work is a formal interrogation of the very nature of fiction.[8]

It is possible that Voussois is Voudzoï, but it is just as possible that he is not; and Pierrot and the reader must play with the possibility of difference as well as of sameness in their construction of meaning. This kind of ambivalence does not mean, however, that Queneau, like some later novelists, excludes the referential world from his novel. For, as I have stressed, Queneau is always ready to give the world's messy heterogeneity its due. In *Pierrot* Queneau creates a referential space to which he admits the most varied forms of popular culture and entertainment as well as a nearly sociological portrait of the margins of society. There is again a festive side to Queneau's delight in popular culture, or his parodistic portrayal of the popular fête. Little in modern fiction can match, for example, the festive aggression with which he describes the "philosophers" and their antics at the fun house, or the fights that these lovers of wisdom get into. Their attack on the fun house gives Queneau the chance to create some of the most burlesque transgression against the language of fiction to be found in his work.

One can, of course, evoke other examples of the modern artist's interest in popular culture: James Joyce or, more broadly, the nineteenth-century tradition in which the artist came to see the circus performer, the clown, and the mountebank as emblems of the artist and his status in developing capitalism. Queneau differs from Joyce and even more so from Baudelaire in that he does not usually present his clowns or performers as allegorical doubles for himself or the artist—the one exception being perhaps Pierre, the magician, performer, and surrogate narrator in *The Bark Tree.* In *Les Derniers Jours,* *A Hard Winter, Pierrot,* and a good many of the later novels Queneau presents movie stars and circus performers, animal trainers and clowns, mediums and voyants, fakirs and freaks, for what they are: comic emblems of real popular culture that can also function metonymically to designate all the heterogeneity that makes up our contemporary world.

The last novel we shall consider in this chapter, *Loin de Rueil* (*The Skin of Dreams*, 1944), makes the movies its focal point, and its hero, Jacques, is both a moviegoer and finally a movie star. Queneau maintained on several occasions that film allows us to project ourselves into the roles of the stars and to fulfill our imaginative fantasies; he also held that the movies had been so interiorized into our consciousness that they now inform our perceptions and even give shape to our dreams. Or as the poet of *The Skin of Dreams* puts it about watching movies, "I'm transported onto the screen by something like a magic act or, in any case, a transcendental one; and I find myself taking consciousness of myself in the form of one of the heroes of the story that's been narrated to us by means of flat but moving images."[9] Des Cigales's description of how film works gives us the basic premise for narration in *The Skin of Dreams:* Queneau has created a comic work in which film roles and dreams, waking fantasies and theatricalized conduct usually are indistinguishable from ordinary waking consciousness. The old philosophical problem of telling appearance from reality has been transformed into the difficulty of distinguishing celluloid fantasies from everyday conduct.

Jacques L'Aumône is the character whose adventures challenge the reader to resolve this modern philosophical dilemma. To give this dilemma a context Queneau has narrated an imaginary film biography of the man who, with his name translated, becomes the American actor James Charity. Queneau begins the novel, however, with the poet Des Cigales, a fellow writer who suffers from asthma or, more precisely, *ontalgie*. This is an existential malady whose name also resembles "ontology," the study of being which is central to existentialist philosophies. Like Daniel in *Les Enfants du Limon*, the poet encounters true being in the anguish of his attacks, when he discovers that he has no more existence than a louse on the globe. Lice, it must be noted, have more than a small place in this work: every chapter in the novel has an obligatory discussion of or reference to Queneau's favored vermin.

Des Cigales is a friend of the L'Aumône family, and in what may or may not be a fantasy projection we learn that this poet of noble birth is Jacques's real father. Acting in what seems to be an adventure film Jacques accepts his noble background and reclaims his royal heritage. But Jacques has multiple identities. At or in a western, in a manner reminiscent of Buster Keaton's *Sherlock, Jr.* (1924), he steps into the screen and promptly starts shooting bad guys while saving the virtuous heroine. And, just as abruptly, the reader finds him with two sisters, Dominique and Camille, ready to teach Camille how they kiss in the movies. These transformations may seem, on the one hand, to be parodies of existentialist desires to privilege concrete states of consciousness by granting them total autonomy: consciousness is the world, no matter how fantastic. On the other hand, Queneau is playing with the way cinema informs consciousness of the world with its projective fantasies. Using abrupt ellipses, rather like cinematic jump cuts with no transitions, Queneau scrambles all codes that might point to different levels of narration, and the reader has no way of differentiating between "real" events in the work and fantasies that characters might be acting out. American readers will find none of this problematic, since Walter Mitty has probably already given them a few pointers on how to negotiate this labyrinth.

The reader must suspend judgment about the "reality" of such events as Jacques's awakening from what appears to be a dream about his musical career; or when he appears to step into a stereotypical boxing movie to become middle-weight champion of the world. Queneau is allowing Jacques to live out the dreams of omnipotence that the movies grant us in their most stereotypical genres, be it westerns or boxing movies. Intercalated with what are or are not fantasies is a recognizable plot. Jacques meets a woman named Suzanne who then reappears as the mother of his child. Jacques nearly fleeces Des Cigales in a scheme to have unknown poets pay to have their works published; and meets Dominique again, this time playing the role of a ticket taker on the trolley. Characters undergo metamorphosis with all the fluidity of Sartrean actors freely taking on different roles.

Jacques apparently dreams his way through university studies, becomes a chemical engineer, though he has also been a dancer and has organized a theatrical troop. Tiring of his project to raise a race of giant lice or to find a cure for *ontalgie,* Jacques runs away from provincial life with the Provinc' Folies, whose star Rojana Pontez is another metamorphosis of Camille. Jacques becomes an actor, or at least a walker-on, in Paris, where he finds Dominique in her latest guise: a rich socialite. Queneau then turns Jacques into a practicing ascetic who, nonetheless, yearns for the charms that Camille's body offers. She refuses him, though Jacques learns from a friend that in other roles she supposedly sleeps around a good deal.

The novel comes to a conclusion with a pastiche of a thirties adventure film when Jacques goes to the tropics to make a documentary. Reuniting a good many of the novel's characters in the Saint James Infirmary Bar of San Culebra de Porco, the novel offers an exotic scene of carousing drawn straight from the coincidence-laden narratives of Hollywood dream-machines. The novel's finale also takes place at the movies, for Des Cigales takes Suzanne and Jacques's son Michou to discover the latest Hollywood sensation, James Charity, an American actor who speaks Rabelaisian French in an interview with a movie magazine. James Charity has become such a popular star that he makes a movie narrating his own life and career—a career crowned by this movie narrating his life. The film, *La Peau des Rêves,* or *The Skin of Dreams,* is an imaginary film telling the novel itself, a novel in which narration about the movies culminates in a movie narrating the novel. None of the characters in France can, however, recognize Jacques in his new role, which is not surprising since even Raymond Queneau becomes, when pronounced with an American accent in Hollywood, Ramon Curnough, Ramon Curnough being naturally the producer of this hit film.

*The Skin of Dreams* ends in typically circular fashion, with a self-representation in miniature at the work's end. Movies and novels are not the only forms of representation that mirror each other in this work, for Queneau refers to a wide spectrum of usually theatrical forms of representation. Jacques begins life as a moviegoer, but he is also involved in dreams of opera, organizes a theater company named after Molière's Illustre Théâtre, performs in music hall spectacles, dances, and, as his final film says, participates in a *roman comique. Roman comique* means a comic novel, which certainly describes *The Skin of Dreams.* This is also the title of the seventeenth-century novel by Scarron, a work told by a comically self-reflexive narrator, who relates the extravagant adventures of a provincial theater troop. In a sense Queneau is updating the *Roman comique* with his festive parody of forms of representation, and through this he is suggesting that movies have now taken the place of other forms of representation that once allowed the public enactment of our fantasies and dreams. *The Skin of Dreams* proposes a comic acknowledgement of the primacy of dreams in those representations of what we consider to be reality.

The world is a stage, but it has also become a silver screen, and on it we watch the metamorphoses of our dreams, and perhaps our lives. The metamorphosis of characters, their fundamental instability, is tied to this primacy of dream in representation, both in *The Skin of Dreams* and in a number of other of Queneau's novels, especially *Zazie in the Metro*. But in *The Skin of Dreams* Queneau comes perhaps closest to being our modern Apuleus or Ovid with the comic mutations that his characters freely undergo. Queneau's vision of metamorphosis is overdetermined, since we sense that he is also parodying the existentialist view that man is a totally free actor. Metamorphosis conveys, in addition, a fundamentally comic vision of an unstable world of appearances in which seeming is being. It is not for nothing that Hamlet, the actor-prince, should be one of Queneau's favorite characters in world literature. For acting is the key metaphor to describe the play of appearance that characterizes man's being and a fortiori the representation of his reality.

But whence the lice? Many readers are likely to find them more perplexing than Queneau's metaphysics of representation. Every episode manages to include a discussion of lice, usually couched in the most banal of formulaic repetitions ("I got mine at school"). The rich friends whom Dominique entertains, for example, limit their conversations to the "usual things": travel, films, and lice. Or in a semifantasy sequence, it is, not surprisingly, at the Bal des Poux—the "Lice Ball"—that Jacques meets a woman who becomes his mistress. Even love can be infected with lice, though of a different species from the usual, the *phtirius pubis,* whose slang equivalent in French, *morpion,* is one of the funnier words in the language. Lice are everywhere.

In comic opposition to Jacques's extraordinary adventures, lice proliferate throughout these episodes like a sign that the fatal fall into the trivially real may come at any moment. Queneau has not left the fall out of this novel, though he has transformed it into an unusual comic leitmotiv. In *The Skin of Dreams* it first appears that we cannot, as psychoanalysis would hold that we can, distinguish fantasy or desire from reality. If the order of the real and the order of desire are inextricably mixed, then no one can decide if Jacques is really a boxer or merely a film addict who dreams of physical omnipotence. But Queneau does allow a certain reality to invade the order of desire, what we might call the "order of lice," that constantly calls us back to the essential banality that, we think, usually has the last word in Queneau's works.

As a form of repetition the theme of lice, like other forms of recurrence and coincidence, also mocks our desire for the genesis of meaning. The absurdity of this recurrence seems especially apt to lay bare our inclination, as well-schooled readers, to seek in all forms of repetition an excess of meaning that goes beyond mere denotation or simple reference. Of course, to read this outbreak of lice as a rather banal example of banality that rules supreme in Queneau's work is to fall, self-consciously we hope, into the trap that Queneau has set for us—for there is nothing more banal than the desire to find meaning everywhere.

To conclude this chapter, let me note that Queneau's last two novels, *Pierrot* and *The Skin of Dreams,* are in many ways much closer to the dominant sensibility of the time of their publication than was Queneau's first novel, or, for that matter, than were *Les Derniers Jours* or *Les Enfants du Limon*. Little in modern fiction, except a knowledge of Joyce, could have prepared the French reading public for *The Bark Tree*. *Pierrot* and *The Skin of Dreams* appeared during the Occupation. For obvious reasons during that time of despair, existentialism was quickly becoming the dominant sensibility in France. *Pierrot* and *The Skin of Dreams,* and especially the latter, are ambivalent in their often parodistic play with the existentialist themes of anguish, freedom, and the absurd. They are nonetheless informed by a sensibility that in the most basic sense accepts the absurd as a fundamental category of existence. That, as we noted, Albert Camus would write for himself a perceptive commentary on *Pierrot* is undoubtedly a sign that Queneau was slowly acquiring some readers, and some rather important ones. Queneau was not, however, content to remain fixed by the era's mood, and in his next work, *Saint Glinglin,* he set forth writing and rewriting a work whose anthropological vision has little precedent in twentieth-century fiction.

## Chapter Five
# The Novels: The Years after World War II

*The Skin of Dreams,* for all its play with fantasy and reality, is a quite accessible novel. We all have familiarity with the dreams of fantastic omnipotence and fulfillment that Hollywood once proposed as the stuff of our desires. The first novel Queneau published after the war, *Saint Glinglin* (1948), is a much more demanding work for a "full" reading, since it enacts an intellectual comedy whose scope of reference includes most of Western anthropological thought and the myths that this anthropology has highlighted in its attempt to understand the nature of culture. For the intellectual framework of the novel Queneau draws on a great range of thinkers, philosophical and anthropological, such as Hegel, Durkheim, Frazer, Mead, Mauss, Rank, and Freud. He also makes intertextual use of writers like Shakespeare, Montesquieu, Swift, and Baudelaire, writers who in their works have made us look upon our own culture through foreign eyes and consider it as something other than nature, as a system that can be viewed at a distance in its alterity and strangeness. In *Saint Glinglin* Queneau invents an imaginary society, not unlike the Swift of *Gulliver's Travels,* that incorporates traits of French and other Western societies. Like the Montesquieu of *The Persian Letters,* he also obliges us to ask how it is possible to belong to a "foreign" culture. However, Swiftian satire is not the principal aim of *Saint Glinglin,* or if there is a satirical intent in this novel, it aims at the anthropological attempt to know culture as much as at the specific traits that make up a given culture.

In a sense *Saint Glinglin* is a trilogy, since Queneau rewrote two earlier works and incorporated them into the novel. *Gueule de Pierre* (1934) serves, though with many stylistic changes, fairly much in its original form as the first part of *Saint Glinglin;* whereas *Temps mêlés* (1941) has been completely rewritten. This process of composition may explain in part why the novel unfolds as seven discrete narrative blocks. Queneau also capitalized on different narrative modes in each section to offer different points of view and to change style and diction as he saw fit. Narration is linear, for the novel follows an imaginary chronology, beginning in "Les Poissons" (The fish) with a first-person narration by Pierre Nabonide. This young man has been sent to the "Foreign City" to learn its language. He cannot, however, learn the "gibberish" that surrounds him and he prefers to spend his days in the city aquarium. Pondering the bizarre aquatic life he finds there, he wonders, for example, how he and a lobster can both be said to share the same category of existence, namely, life. Pierre shows himself to have the makings of a Hegelian categorizer of the first order.

Pierre comes from the "Native City" where his father, the mayor, has sequestered Pierre's sister. His brother Jean writes him from the Arid Mountain that there will be changes this year in the city's annual festival, "Saint Glinglin," a fictitious saint's day meaning "never" in popular French. The festival is described in the second part, "Le Printanier," Queneau's name for the spring potlach to which all the city's inhabitants contribute enormous amounts of crockery and porcelain, which they then destroy with great relish, Mayor Nabonide leading the way with a machine gun. The ensuing fête demands great consumption of alcoholic *fifrequet* and *brouchtou-caille,* a Rabelaisian stew for which Queneau gives the recipe in a parody of an ethnologist's sense of exactitude. Pierre returns on the day of the fête to give a discourse on Life, but his father intervenes and deprives him of the right to speak.

Anthropological motifs abound in the second section as well as in the following. Nabonide resembles the father of Freud's primal hoard, since he obviously wants to keep all the women to himself. As in the myth Freud concocted for *Totem and Taboo,* the sons revolt; and in the third section "Le Caillou" (The pebble) Jean narrates in nearly biblical verse the father's demise when, pursued by the sons, he falls into the Petrifying Spring. Pierre has resisted his father's attempt to "castrate" him and returns from the mountain with his "truth of stone"—the stone Father—that he, now the new mayor, places in the City like a megalith or perhaps a deity.

Pierre's other brother, Paul, takes up the narration in "Les Rur-aux" (The country dwellers) in order to perorate against the coun-tryside and nature, detestable regions that have no meaning as they endlessly repeat the same patterns. Meaning can only be found in the city, with its newly imported "cinematograph." Paul has fallen in love with the star "Alice Phaye," and the transformations she brings to the City—girdles and brassieres—represent a triumph of culture over mere nature.

The fifth section, "Les Touristes" (The tourists), sees foreign travelers come to the City in the persons of Alice Phaye and an "ethnographer." Queneau seems to be recalling that the first ethnographers were those tourists who brought back descriptions of non-European cultures. This ethnographer arrives at a crucial moment, for the new mayor is going to abolish the festival. He is also planning to get rid of the beautiful weather that has always existed, and bring about the reign of wetness. The Native City's culture undergoes fundamental change when rain does fall, dissolving the Father's statue, and provoking the angry populace so that they sack Pierre for having brought foreign ideas into their land. And the ethnographer learns that the *chasse-nuages* or "cloud-chaser" of the City's lore must not have been a myth after all.

The sister Hélène narrates the sixth section, "Les Etrangers" (The foreigners), during her sequestration in a foreign land. Surrounded by vermin to which she gives names, she speaks a mad interior monologue that Gilbert Pestureau sees as a parody of Faulkner (such as Benjy's monologue at the beginning of *The Sound and the Fury*).[1] It is also a kind of anthropological satire of Western culture. She describes the foreign culture surrounding her in terms of its obsession with papers: one can give oneself an identity with them, exchange them against food, or wipe oneself with the same. Moreover, everything is organized in the foreign city in *boîtes* (meaning "boxes," "cans," and "buildings"): one is born in them, lives in them, is buried in them, and can find food in them. Hélène's monologue is a satirical linguistic anthropology, showing that, at least through wordplay, all elements of culture can be described in terms of every other.

The final chapter, "Saint Glinglin," presents the return of the festival and the beautiful weather, the expulsion of foreign cultural traits, and perhaps an escape from historical change. The central issue here is Queneau's mocking demonstration of how historical legends take shape when Jean becomes a scapegoat for the City and plays out his role as a shaman. A Shakespearean conspiracy of disgruntled citizens is under way; and revolt is imminent when Paul, having become mayor, changes the fête again. He has Alice Phaye, now his wife, swim in scant attire before the populace. Jean then takes expiation upon himself and demands that a *nasse* (an eel pot or lobster trap) be imported. The importer receives instead a *manche à air* (airfield wind-scoop). The City's populace cannot tell the difference, and Jean is placed in what they take to be the lobster trap and hoisted into the sky. The wind blows, the sun comes out, and Jean dries into a mummy. The fête of Saint Glinglin is restored in his honor, even as a new statue of the Father melts in the sun. The populace believes it knows again how to control the weather, for it now has a new founding myth upon which to base its belief in its power over nature. Sacrifice, in a sense the anthropologist Mauss would have understood, has led to profound modifications of society. Queneau has shown the reader that both lobster and lobster trap can be the elements that change as well as restore society. This wacky conclusion parodies the need to ascribe origins to culture. It may even show that the supposed restoration of origins always demands a founding myth of sacrifice.

At the heart of Queneau's travesty is a questioning of the basic conceptuality with which we think about culture and nature, biology and anthropology. In his alienated way Pierre is the naive observer who discovers that linguistic taxonomies arbitrarily group together things that appear to have no commonality. Looking at aquatic worms and at himself, he longs to find a conceptual system that would satisfactorily organize the human and the inhuman in ways that account for obvious appearances. Pierre asks questions such as what is the measure of commensurability between a man and all the inhuman creatures that nature takes pleasure in multiplying; or, for that matter, between a man who speaks the Native Language and the incomprehensible foreigners with their gibberish. Neither biological nor anthropological categories seem to be able to account for otherness or difference.

If a Hegelian need to find a totalizing system is reflected in Pierre's anguish, it must be said that the categories for nature that he comes up with—such as Terror, Silence, and Darkness—seem to be more existentialist than Hegelian in nature, or at least a comic facsimile thereof. Queneau directly travesties existentialism when Pierre discovers that a privileged emotion gives him access to truth about "eksistence." This emotion is not Heidegger's angst or Sartre's nausea; rather it is vertigo that opens the way to a comprehension of "eggistence." Vertigo reveals, one might say, the arbitrary nature of linguistic classifications that classify Pierre and a lobster with the same rubric. The first part of *Saint Glinglin* enacts a remarkable satire of the desire to find categories and concepts that would exactly delimit their referents within a totalizing system. Which is not to say that Queneau does not make us feel a malaise about the arbitrary categories that we often believe, when talking about nature or culture, to be inherent in some nature of things. The bizarre and the weird are also categories, at least for all too human humans such as Pierre.

After Hegel, Heidegger, and taxonomic thought in general, Freud and the Bible provide *Saint Glinglin* with some of its principal motifs. Queneau had already attempted in *Chêne et chien* to forge a countermyth that would displace the patriarchial vision of logos that underwrites the Judeo-Christian tradition as well as the transmission of the law in the manner that psychoanalysis conceives this process. With the prophet-brother Jean and the revolt against the father Queneau again makes allusion to the common biblical-psychoanalytic view of culture, with quite specific use of Freud's *Totem and Taboo*. Jean's speaking in biblical verses, to narrate the revolt of the sons against the father, underscores Queneau's view that Freud's myth of the foundation of society is essentially the same as the Bible's. Both myths depend on an originating act of violence: the ritual murder of the father whose word is the source of law (Christianity's version is the Father who immolates himself as the Son). All of these motifs, though in no systematic fashion, circulate throughout *Saint Glinglin*. Ironic distortions rather than systematic allusions are the rule, such as the petrification of the father, which, in a comic way, might reflect the Judaic version of the bestowal of the Father's word on stone tablets. The point here finally is not so much a systematic parody of either Freud or the Judeo-Christian tradition, but of attempts to categorize cultures with motifs that are themselves products of the culture that would do the classifying.

Pierre imposes against his father his "vérité de pierre" (in a play on words, his "truth in stone"), which marks, as Paul observes, the City's entrance into a "historical epoch." Paul is a pointed cultural observer, though with a decided bias. His diatribe against nature springs from his view that nature is outside history, and therefore it can have no meaning for the human mind. Nature endlessly repeats the same natural signs; it is, as he says, an "infinite pleonasm." This hatred of nature's meaningless redundancy is inspired to a large degree by the Baudelaire of *Les Peintres de la vie moderne* (The painters of modern life). Baudelaire took malicious pleasure in castigating those eighteenth-century thinkers who believed in the goodness of nature, since it was obvious to Baudelaire that nature could only recall man's fall. Culture is the history of man's attempt to overcome nature, which is to say his fall, and this overcoming can only take place in the city. Paul's dithyrambs on girdles and brassieres are a humorously Baudelairean form of praise of man's capacity to perfect nature (and for the Baudelairean misogynist woman is nature). For Paul, as for Baudelaire, culture is beyond nature, and all historical forms of culture—philosophy, religion, art, and, Paul would add, the movies—are attempts to transcend man's fall.

With the introduction of his ethnographer, Dussouchel, Queneau brings a European scientific observer onto the scene, though this anthropologist is more interested in the legs of a local girl than in the natives' customs. Doussouchel is obliged to take note of some local mores, however; for instance, when the leaders of the conspirators demonstrate the regards to which tourists are entitled: strong kicks in the rear. Queneau never hesitates to use Rabelaisian farce to create what we might call his own potlatch, one aiming at the festive destruction of cultural forms, in this case those forms by which we think we have knowledge of culture. Dussouchel is emblematic in this respect, for his scientific inquiry is a farcical enterprise in which the observer is as libidinously caught up in the scene he would observe as are the local residents.

Through this farce Queneau asks how any observer can see the otherness or alterity of another culture. Anthropology has claimed this can be done by identifying discrete cultural traits and matching their sameness and difference from one culture to another. Queneau plays with this model, showing it to be based on an impossible dialectic in which the same can only be identified as difference, and vice versa. The inhabitants of the Native City are utterly different from us, and yet they have all the essential traits of the pleasure-seeking petty bourgeois whose traits we identify through our knowledge of our European culture. They speak those essential clichés that the anthropologist Malinowski called phatic language, but which look like the banalities of our everyday discourse.

Anthropology also proposes that we can trace the diffusion of culture by tracing the spread of cultural traits or institutions. Queneau duly notes the arrival of cultural "difference" into the Native City; not only in the form of such an institution as the movies, and the accompanying female apparel, but also later in such "traits" as *protège-pluies* and *ouateurproofes*—neologisms for such obviously foreign "institutions" as umbrellas and raincoats. The latter are necessitated, of course, by the arrival of that new historical situation, unending rain. Rain has arrived thanks to Pierre's contamination with foreignness, and thus it appears that nature itself can be contaminated by cultural institutions. With this demonstration Queneau has again, with festive farce, obliterated those conceptual distinctions like "nature" and "culture" with which we organize our understanding of the world.

Finally, Queneau's work plays with a myth that has been central to anthropological thought from Hegel through Freud and which still organizes some supposedly scientific thought about man. That myth is framed in terms of a study of the origins of society and culture. The belief in an origin is a clear case of the desire to explain the observable by the unobservable, the known by the unknown. Much of Queneau's fiction is a meditation on the impossibility of Hegel, and in *Saint Glinglin* this meditation turns on the parody of the notions of historical origins and development. In a sense Queneau sketches an outline familiar to students of anthropology in that the Native City evolves from a prehistorical state through a period of historical development in which change occurs: it rains. At the end the Native City returns, or progresses, to another ahistorical state. One's view of the conclusion will depend on whether one sees this as typical circular return, in which history is abolished with the farcical sacrifice that ends time; or whether one sees Queneau presenting a society that arrives at that stage beyond history, at the end of time, when in Hegelian terms there is no longer historical development (at least according to Kojève's interpretation of Hegel in the lectures that Queneau edited). Both seem plausible; parody is surely at work in either case. I would stress that Queneau's parody, with wordplay and puns, aims primarily at those legends that seek to codify the myth of origins—and by this I mean both the myths themselves and the anthropological systems that would categorize types of origins and development.

Before continuing with Queneau's Hegelian fiction in the next novel he published under his own name, *The Sunday of Life* (1952), I will consider two novels that he published under the pseudonym of Sally Mara: *On est toujours trop bon avec les femmes* (*We Always Treat Women Too Well,* 1947) and Sally's "diary," her *Journal intime* (1950).

The first was published as a translation from the Gaelic by a Michel Presle; whereas the second was offered as a work written by the young Irishwoman, in French, during the thirties. In 1962 Queneau published the two works together as *Les Oeuvres complètes de Sally Mara.* He edited these "complete works" under his own name, though with a Borgesian sense of irony he allowed his fictional Sally to preface the work, specifically to deny authorship of *Foutaises,* a series of quite outlandish puns, that Queneau appended as a third section of the "complete works."

It appears that, much like his friend Boris Vian, Queneau wrote these pseudonymous works because he was asked to furnish some erotic fiction for a new pulp series, Les Editions du Scorpion. After the war this series specialized in the kind of semipornographic and violent fiction to which Americans were already accustomed in their hard-boiled thrillers. Especially in *We Always Treat Women Too Well,* one encounters a mixture of sex and violence that is unique in Queneau's work—even if the characters have names taken from Joyce's *Ulysses.* It is unlikely, however, that anyone who bought the original paperback would have noticed the allusions to Joyce.

In Sally's first novel Queneau describes a fictional siege during the Easter rebellion of 1916 in Dublin after seven Irish revolutionaries seize an imaginary post office. Having shot a functionary and having seized the necessary supplies of Guinness and whiskey, they discover that a Miss Gerty Girdle has become their prisoner while using the lavatory. In the course of the ensuing siege Miss Girdle gives her virginity to one rebel, then takes on another, performs fellatio on a third (only to witness his head blown off while satisfying him), and is finally sodomized by two homosexual members of the band. In the meantime, like Hemingway's men at war, the rebels fight, eat, smoke, drink, and are blown to smithereens. This outline suggests what a reader in 1947 might have gotten from the book if he or she were reasonably subtle, since Queneau's descriptions of sexual matters are rarely graphic, and his language demands at times a kind of decoding, proceeding as it does by indirection. This may be why the work had little success.

Today's reader may pick up the novel's allusions to Joyce and a host of other members of our literary pantheon and still wonder why Queneau wrote this book. Queneau provides a partial answer in *Bâtons, chiffres et lettres* (168–70). Here Queneau reprints his commentary on a popular novel by James Hadley Chase, *No Orchards for Miss Blandish,* in which a young woman is held prisoner by some gangsters and who, despite the torture she undergoes, falls in love with one of her tormentors. Writing in 1944 Queneau stigmatized this sadism as springing from a fascist mentality and noted the paradox that this literature should provide enjoyment for the same democratic people who were then combating fascism. This commentary has caused some critics to assume that in *We Always Treat Women Too Well* Queneau is attempting to defuse sensationalism by a kind of redundancy of effects. In her introduction to Barbara Wright's translation, for example, Valerie Caton maintains that the work is "a calculated act of literary sabotage" designed to show that scenes of sex and violence are not titillating, but are disquieting and absurd.[2] Such reasoning is cogent, but readers who have read the original pulp edition, published with no sign of Queneau's authorship, may well feel that the ironic distancing devices Queneau uses do not offset the fascination of sheer gore, such as when the rebel's head is shot off. The rebels parody Dostoyevski; "Finnegans Wake" is their password; but deciphering Queneau's eroticism is also entertaining in its own right.

In Sally's *Journal intime* the reader supposedly finds a diary by the woman who, as the fiction has it, later writes her only novel in Gaelic. As the diary shows, she has mastered French, though not exactly all the nuances of the language, since she is constantly innocent of the sexual meanings of words. This "diary" is something of an extended gag about her coming to understand the language, and hence the world of sexuality. Queneau is also playing with stereotypes: typically Irish, Sally is ignorant of sex, learns Gaelic out of patriotism, and lives in a family in which whiskey is served at table like milk. She spends much of her time pondering the mysteries of the male crotch. Other "mysteries" include her sister's enjoyment of the frequent spankings her father gives her, or that her brother could be the father of the cook's child without their being married. Queneau multiplies absurd and often hilarious events that relate tangentially to Sally's progress, with Irish, British, and French cultural traits receiving a good many satirical jabs.

Perhaps the linguistic humor of Sally's diary and progress can best be illustrated by noting that the work is framed by a play on words. At the novel's beginning, after the departure of Sally's French tutor, Michel Presle, Sally writes that she was on the docks, wandering in fog, admiring the "rigidity of the bitts" (cable posts, or *bittes,* but *bite* is French slang for penis) when a man calls out to her to hang on to the banister, "Tenez bon la rampe."[3] She then finds in her hand a most agreeably hard and yet soft support. At the novel's end, as she leaves on her honeymoon trip with her rather banal husband, she receives the same command: "I advanced my hand in the darkness, but only found a wet and cold rope. I understood that my conjugal life had just begun" (190). With this discovery of the difference between the figurative and the literal meaning of words, Sally's education is sadly complete.

There is great humor in this work, partly because Sally seems to be at least partly complicitous in this wordplay. She announces that she is a "virgin," which would seem to show that she has some knowledge of the mysteries of the organism. But then she writes that she knows this because she finds in the dictionary the one possible meaning of the term *virgin* that, she thinks, describes her, to wit, "never exploited." She has never been exploited therefore. . . . She meditates hilariously on the literal meaning of words that are clearly used in a figurative sense, as when she finds out that her brother has been "mounting" *(grimper)* the cook and imagines that he must climb up on her shoulders in order to look for a jar of marmalade on an upper shelf. And she slyly recognizes the obsessive nature of her fascination with male anatomy: "I mustn't let my eyes always be wandering about on male citizens' parts and allow that to become an obsession and then fall into some sort of mysticism with phallucinations" (46). Through Sally Queneau is making sport of the very notion of naïveté and the possibility of using language in ways that systematically avoid sexual reference. With systematic avoidance one makes of course systematic reference, and does indeed run the risk of "phallucinations."

Taken together the two novels composing Sally's "complete works" represent Queneau's foray into a nearly literal writing of popular fiction. The gags, parodies, erudite allusions, and the extravagance of the plots, especially in the *Journal intime,* could suggest Queneau was using popular genres in order to undermine them. One confronts, however, the same problems in these works, especially in *We Always Treat Women Too Well,* that recent art works using "pop" genres have posed to us: to what extent does the pop art of a Warhol, a Lichtenstein, or, in cinema, a Godard, ironically undermine its pop models and to what extent does it affirm their values or ideological status? For Queneau's novel about Irish rebels is not unlike

Lichtenstein's literal imitation of a cartoon strip, and Lichtenstein's is a form of pop art that is quite ambivalent in its attitude toward the violence that it glorifies.

In another perspective we would also suggest that Queneau is playing ironically with sexual stereotypes in fiction, such as they are portrayed in pop culture for the male and female imagination. In *We Always Treat Women Too Well*, supposedly narrated by a woman, we find a male adventure tale that highlights sadistic treatment of women, titillation based on violence, and a pessimistic recognition of the destruction that women inevitably wreak upon men. In the *Journal intime* one can see a kind of parody of the pop fiction that makes appeal to the feminine sense of the pornographic. Titillation is achieved through hints, suggestions, and veiled (or not so veiled) allusions, all centering on constant "phallucinations," the implicit referent of the pulp romance and confessions that aim at a feminine market. Ironically, but appropriately, this novel, like much pulp fiction written for women, was written by a man.

Five years before Queneau published his next signed novel, *Le Dimanche de la vie (The Sunday of Life)*, in 1952, he had published the lectures Kojève had given in the thirties as an introduction to Hegel. Kojève returned the favor when the novel was published by writing an essay on Queneau for the review *Critique*. Kojève interpreted the novel's hero Valentin Brû as the very embodiment of Hegel's posthistorical sage. He saw in Queneau's central character an example of a man enjoying total consciousness and thus total satisfaction with himself as he lives "the Sunday of life" that comes after the end of history. This interpretation may strike some readers as strange, since Valentin Brû seems at first view to be the prototype of the petty bourgeois merchant. In his absorption with his daily pleasures and routines, he looks more like a vehicle for satire than a representative of Absolute Mind. Yet Queneau does open the book with a quotation from Hegel's lectures on aesthetics that suggests that the book has a number of dimensions: "it is the Sunday of life, which levels everything and rejects everything bad; men gifted with such good humor cannot be fundamentally bad or base."[4] Hegel refers here to those seventeenth-century Dutch merchants that Dutch painting has made familiar to us all. But, as Kojève observed, Valentin Brû cannot be situated in these historical terms, since, coming after Hegel supposedly ended history, he must live on the other side of history, when Absolute Mind has come to consciousness of itself.

A brief overview of the events in his life makes clear, moreover, that Brû is not entirely a typical member of his social class. The novel begins when a middle-aged tradeswoman, Julie—sometimes Julia—a *mercière* or notions dealer to be exact, decides that she wants to marry a handsome young soldier—Valentin Brû—about whom she knows absolutely nothing. With help from her sister-in-law, Julie does marry him, but does not accompany him on their honeymoon. Business will not allow it. Valentin travels for both of them, which permits Queneau to concentrate on Valentin's daffy adventures in Paris when he gets lost, is fleeced by a taxi driver, fleeces him in his turn, and on the return leg of his trip follows an anonymous funeral procession (in a bit of self-parody that also evokes Shakespeare and Jules Romain). The funeral is coincidentally for the deceased lover of Julie's sixty-seven-year-old mother.

Upon the mother's death Valentin inherits a shop in the twelfth *arrondissement* in Paris. Ostensibly a dealer in picture frames, Valentin spends much of his time staring at a clock or talking with the neighbors. Without her husband's knowing it, Julie becomes a medium and uses Valentin's access to gossip as a solid base for the predictions she peddles. When she becomes ill, she suggests to Valentin that he replace her as "Madame Sophie," which he does with rather good success. History, however, brings about a general mobilization for a war with Germany that no one has believed possible, except Valentin Brû. Finding himself back in provincial barracks life while waiting for the war to begin, Valentin, "a benign atheist," decides to become a saint. Since the name "Valentin" also seems to allude to a Gnostic heretic much despised by early church fathers, one could predict his failure, all the more so in that Valentin really prefers the joys of the flesh to those of the spirit. Such is the sense of the novel's final scene when Julie, looking for her husband in a train station after the French defeat, sees Valentin helping some girls climb into a train through a window—and taking advantage of the opportunity to feel their buttocks.

Returning to Kojève's perhaps ironic Hegelian reading of *The Sunday of Life,* the reader may well ask where is Hegel in all this, and the question is quite to the point. Queneau's recurrent allusions to Hegel usually try to show that philosophical systems are incapable of accounting for ordinary human events, especially those periods

of life that are happy. Or perhaps there is a comic coincidence here
between Hegel's absurdly logical point of view that history ended
with his philosophy and Queneau's view, as expressed in *Une Histoire
modèle,* that there can be no history of happiness, only of unhappiness.
For happiness never inaugurates change, but only continues the
little pleasures of an essentially petty bourgeois existence. The end
of history would coincide with an era of petty bourgeois hedonism.
True history, on the other hand, is brought about by the predictable
recurrence of catastrophes that produce change. In *The Sunday of
Life,* then, Queneau chooses not to portray history.

It is remarkable that in *The Sunday of Life* Queneau has written
a work in which history, understood as unhappy events initiating
change, is constantly alluded to, but never shown. The reader learns
that Valentin Brû participated in the French campaign to subdue
rebellious tribes in Madagascar, and Madagascar is referred to
throughout the novel without the reader ever learning what Valentin
did there. The forthcoming war with Germany is predicted—and
gainsaid—throughout the novel, but when it comes, Queneau skips
over it to conclude the book with a comic image of human foibles.
Valentin's foibles may well represent the substance of happiness. In
short, history is absent from the novel, which must be the case if
one is enjoying the Sunday of life. Does this mean that Valentin's
enjoyment of wine, sauces, and sex is on the other side of history?
Or should one see a parody of Hegel in Valentin's living outside
history, especially since Valentin's greatest desire in life is to visit
the battlefield at Jena? It was at Jena that Hegel saw in Napoleon's
victory over the Prussians the march of the "spirit of history" that
was bringing about the completion of history; or, as it has been
said, German philosophy was given teeth by a French sword. Valentin does visit Jena, but this trip, organized by the Germans, turns
out to be a propaganda effort. It begins with visits to scenes of
French victories and ends with sightseeing on the fields of Prussian
victories, which is Queneau's demonstration that the Nazis did not
see history as completed at all.

Valentin's meditating on the battle of Jena, like Pierrot's reflections on the death of Louis XIV, is really a concern with nothing.
Valentin also tries to seize nothing when he sees how long he can
concentrate on watching the movement of the long hand of a clock.
Parodying Husserl's lectures on the phenomenology of time (and
perhaps Einstein's definition of time), these vacuous meditations on

a clock also recall Hegel's definition that mind is time, for mind realizes itself through its history, or so Hegel put it in his Jena lectures. History for Valentin lasts about four minutes, since this is his maximum performance in transforming his consciousness into consciousness of time, and thus history.

History is also knowledge, certain knowledge of the past, which, if it were a science, should also grant predictive knowledge of the future. Valentin Brû does not believe in prophets, but he knows war will come. Given Queneau's view of history as the cyclical recurrence of unhappiness, the statement that "war will occur" is bound to be correct, for the repetition of unhappiness seems to have a degree of probability approaching certainty. More comically interesting are Madame Sophie's predictions of those individual events that punctuate the Sunday of life. She see in a fulgurant vision that a neighbor will die. After he becomes a seer, Valentin also speculates: having seen another neighbor between two gendarmes, he wonders if this event signified that the neighbor would murder his wife. But Valentin comes to the conclusion that this predictive knowledge is utterly useless: "Julie might have told Madame Verterelle, too, that she *would* die in bed. But he, Valentin, what would he have been able to tell Madame Virole and Madame Verterelle? That they would win in the lottery and that they'd live to be a hundred and twenty in a villa on the Côte d'Azur? That would have pleased them, but it wouldn't have prevented them from kicking the bucket" (148). Valentin sees that certain knowledge of the future is about as fruitful, Queneau might say, as Hegel's certain knowledge of the past. Some events happen because they must happen, and knowing their certainty is as useful as knowing some events in the past had to happen, simply because they did happen.

Valentin gains in knowledge, not necessarily predictive knowledge, as the novel progresses. He discovers that voiced words and conscious states do not necessarily coincide. People can lie. Valentin's psychological development is, however, of secondary interest, for, like Pierrot, Valentin is another carnival figure that Queneau uses as a kind of mask in order to travesty the world of high seriousness, largely through an inversion of appearances. Consider in this regard Valentin's desire to be a street sweeper or his attraction to brooms. Sweeping is Queneau's solution to the world's fallenness and is a perennial task in a world of unrelenting garbage. The street sweeper is also a traditional figure of carnival; and comic sweeping

embodies the carnivalesque desire for purification and renewal, and
to rid the world of the dust of crumbling structures that collapse
before the rejuvenating power of laughter.

In the same vein in which Valentin desires to be a street sweeper
he also takes on the task of being a saint. In a sense street sweepers
are our secular saints who take upon themselves the world's fall into
muck in order to purify it. Queneau's love of comic incongruity
allows him to combine in Valentin the mock ascetic and the petty
bourgeois lover of food, his sister-in-law, and young girls' buttocks.
Of course, the carnival saint is the travesty figure who, as in Rabelais,
affirms the vanity of the world so as to be able to drink all the more
or to lower his pants in lewd affirmation of the nether parts of the
body. There is, to recall the quotation from Hegel, nothing base
here; but rather the affirmation of the innocent materiality of life
in the here and now.

This carnivalesque sense of travesty circulates throughout the
novel in the various ways the work flaunts its own fictional nature
at every level of reading. One of the most comic devices is Queneau's
use of a different spelling every time he mentions Valentin's brother-
in-law, Paul Butaga, Brébagra, Bradégat, etc. The letter *B* acts like
a changing mask to designate characters throughout the novel, not
the least of which is Brû. At a different level the explicit intertextual
play with Hegel, as well as the not-so-explicit allusions to the heretic
Valentinus and Gnostic heresy, also maintains an awareness of the
fiction as fiction, or of writing as self-conscious play with other
texts. Perhaps the main irony in this regard, however, is the general
structural irony that pervades the entire novel. The reader knows
that he is reading a novel that Queneau published in 1952. The
ironic convention here demands, however, that the reader suppose
that the narration is advancing in time toward the French defeat in
1940. But the novel feigns to be ignorant of the future, even if
Valentin Brû offers accurate prophecy about the coming of the war.
Retrospectively, of course, this is certain knowledge, and, again
retrospectively, the novel appears to unfold according to "historical
necessity." This irony lays bare the conditions of certainty: certainty
can only exist as a project of writing the past as if it were obeying
some necessity. History shows itself to be another literary game,
but one that often masks its own rules.

But Queneau gives the world, if not history, its due, and this
again in the form of a satire of that petty bourgeois world that

recurs throughout his work. *The Sunday of Life* offers perhaps his most remarkable satire, portraying those mores that once constituted what was most French about France, or what Roland Barthes in another context baptized *francité*.[5] In Julie/Julia, for instance, we find that sense of propriety that allows one to tease a customer about her husband's incredible sexual capacity, but which calls for an outburst of obscenities when a waiter calls her "Mademoiselle," thus implying that the man with her is not legally entitled to climb on top of her. Her avarice, her envy of others' success, and her willingness to predict catastrophes for those who are getting ahead are among those traits that all are willing to attribute to that wonderful monster, the French petty bourgeois. It is not a bitter satire that Queneau proposes, for he has no interest in proposing a superior morality by which the world might gain salvation. Rather, he delights in the contradictions of a worldview that, much like Hegelian philosophy, can parody itself. Yet, as in Hegelian philosophy, there is a certain logic to it all: one cannot put off a honeymoon trip until vacation time, Julie correctly reasons, for if one did, when would one take a vacation?

*The Sunday of Life* ends with Valentin Brû about to take a train, and Queneau's next work, *Zazie in the Metro* (1959), begins with its nubile protagonist arriving by train in Paris. To refer to trains in fiction is usually to make reference to a real means of transportation that exists in the world, and in Valentin Brû's case the train is there to keep his fiction within the limits of the real (as well as to provide an occasion for other satisfactions). *Zazie,* however, is a novel in which reality is constantly denied, at least to the foul-mouthed child who wishes to see Paris mainly in order to see the underground train called the Metro. The Metro is on strike, and so is the reality principle in this novel in which a comic play of metamorphosis constantly subverts its referential framework. This subversion takes the form of numerous verbal transgressions and parodies as well as through travesties of the notion of identity. Parallels with *The Skin of Dreams* are plentiful, though in *Zazie* there is no interference between dream and reality, or celluloid fantasies and some reality exterior to those fantasies. From the moment Zazie steps onto the quay, she is an aggressive force that turns the world topsy-turvy. Literature and the language of literature are, in part, the target of this young lady's obscene refrains, but so are the notions of cultural limits encoded in language. *Zazie* is another carnivalesque celebration of the destruction of holy pieties.

Zazie has been entrusted to her uncle Gabriel, since her mother assumes that this giant female impersonator, married to the sweet "Marceline," will not try to rape her child. On the trip to Gabriel's apartment neither Gabriel nor his taxi driver friend Charles can tell the Panthéon from the Gare de Lyon. The reader cannot be sure if these tourist guides are utter nincompoops, or if the French capital has lost its moorings as if in dream—or perhaps both. The theme of the absurdity of tourism is a favorite of Queneau's; and here it is baroquely tied up with the possibility of the oneiric transformation of the Parisian landscape. Gabriel is a tutu-wearing cicerone who has escaped from Calderon's *Life Is a Dream.*

Escaping from her uncle the morning after her arrival, Zazie is nearly caught by his friend, the café proprietor Turandot, but she transforms a crowd that gathers around them by claiming that Turandot was making obscene propositions to her. The titillated crowd wants to hear all, and in the excitement Zazie escapes again, this time to meet another carnivalesque master in metamorphosis, the mysterious Pedro Surplus, who is perhaps a cop, perhaps a lecher, and whom she inveigles into buying her a pair of U.S. Army surplus blue jeans. However, Pedro cannot be escaped, and when she tries the same trick on him she pulled on Turandot, he transforms the crowd by claiming she has stolen the jeans. Nymphet meets satyr in a comic dual of enchantment.

After returning to Gabriel's apartment, Pedro puts in question Gabriel's sexual identity, and Zazie spends the rest of the work asking what a "hormosessual" might be. Pedro himself has no firm identity. Visiting the next-door shoemaker, he claims that he never learned his name by heart. Tourism continues, however, and Charles and Gabriel take Zazie to the Eiffel Tower. Here they are carried away by a bus full of tourists who decide that Gabriel will be their "arch-guide" for a trip to the Sainte-Chapelle. Gabriel is "guide-napped," but Zazie escapes and encounters another version of Pedro in the cop Trouscaillon, who is now pursued by the man-hunting widow Mouacque. Trouscaillon stops a car to pursue the tourists and happens upon a native from Zazie's village who is going at that moment to the Sainte-Chapelle. Coincidence is again the stuff of dreams and fictions.

The tourists may or may not have seen the Sainte-Chapelle; their official guide, Fedor Balanovitch, a phony Russian, says it was the Tribunal de Commerce. The tourists seem not to care, for they take delight in a repast of rotten food by which Queneau satirizes French cuisine while celebrating an inverted festive banquet. Gabriel proposes more typical Parisian tourism when he invites all to come see him dance at the gay nightclub where he works. Except for "Marceline," all come to the fête, including Turandot's Shakespearean parrot whose refrain is a bit of self-reflexive commentary for the entire novel: "Talk, talk that's all you can do." Gabriel demonstrates his "art," while, in a bit of parallel montage, Pedro-Trouscaillon, now naming himself after the Paris street Bertin Poirée, sets about to abuse sweet "Marceline." With allusion to Jacques Prévert and Marcel Carné's film about the devil, Pedro is also called a "visitor of the evening." His other diabolical ancestors must include at least Bébé Toutout and Mephistopheles. After giving him a grammar lesson, "Marceline" flees.

The novel's slapdash conclusion is another of Queneau's homages to cinematic metamorphosis. Trouscaillon appears at the party, is arrested by two cops, who, à la Buster Keaton, are all arrested in turn by other cops. Zazie falls asleep when the group goes to the nightclub "aux Nyctalopes" (or "sufferers of night blindness"). Here ensues a massive brawl, inspired by saloon fights from western movies, in which Gabriel bashes heads and inflicts defeat upon an incredible number of bad guys. Pedro returns, this time as Aroun Arachide, with armored divisions, and a shoot-out takes place that leaves the good widow Mouacque with a stomach-full of bullets. With all the timing of Batman a character appears—"Marceline"— who leads away the beleaguered band, through a goods elevator, into the sewers and through the Metro, to freedom. Zazie, however, sleeps through her only encounter with the underground.

The next day Zazie's mother meets Gabriel's wife, whom she calls "Marcel," and takes the train with her sleepy charge. As for Zazie, she has, she declares, grown older.

Aging is perhaps the only normal trait Queneau attributes to a character in *Zazie,* for verisimilitude is the least of his interests. His characters are again masks, presenting travesties of the received notion of a unified character. Gabriel is a massive giant, perfumed with "Barbouze by Fior," whose profession is to masquerade as a female ballet dancer. This incongruity is an infringement of the

grotesque body upon a realm of grace that we usually accord high
seriousness. A male who plays a female, Gabriel is the very emblem
of the festive inversion of this high seriousness. His carnivalesque
"profession" is a form of inversion that is paralleled by the doubts
one may entertain about his sexual identity. To these uncertain
marks of identity Queneau adds another trait, which is to grant
Gabriel the capacity to speak the language of literature. With all
the suddenness of a Shakespearean hero starting a soliloquy, his
voice can inflate with rhetoric of received cultural codes. He can be
another Hamlet, though echoing Jean-Paul Sartre, when he proclaims that "Being or nothingness, that is the question."[6] He is
also a baroque figure, conscious of his role in a novel proclaiming:
"Paris is but a dream, Gabriel is but a reverie (a charming one),
Zazie the dream of a reverie (or of a nightmare) and all this story
the dream of a dream, the reverie of a reverie, scarcely more than
the typewritten delirium of an idiotic novelist (oh! sorry)" (100).
As this comic metacommentary shows, Gabriel can speak as a literary
critic, a skeptical philosopher, and a theatrical character. He is also
a spokesman for Queneau's view that comedy—*rigolade*—demands
art, for merely donning a tutu does not suffice to make the audience
laugh. All these identities are held together by Gabriel's physical
being: the giant body that recalls the essential materiality of the
world.

The antispiritual, giant body of comedy and carnival has its
medieval antecedents that Rabelais made such good use of in his
creation of giants. Rabelais also made use of the medieval tradition
of devils, those *diables* who made people thirsty by throwing salt in
their mouths, when he created Panurge. Queneau confronts his good
giant with a Mephisto that represents Queneau's most systematic
exploitation of the tradition of comic devils, especially insofar as
Pedro Surplus incarnates the diabolic principle of metamorphosis.
At the novel's end he proclaims that "je suis je" (I am I) and asserts
the very principle of identity that his transformations seem to defy.
Perhaps this is his most diabolic trait, to be constantly the same
while transforming himself at each encounter. Remaining the same
and always different, he is Pedro Surplus, whose very name suggests
the excess of meaning or identity that goes beyond any fixed category
one might attribute to him, except the principle of identity that
allows one to speak of the same identity perduring at the heart of
each metamorphosis. His other names are also suggestive. Trous-

caillon sounds like an homage to Rabelais, whereas Bertin Poirée, though a street, might be an allusion to Agatha Christie's detective Poirot. Aroun Arachide is a deformation of Harun Al Rachid, the caliph of *A Thousand and One Nights.* By these allusions Queneau recalls that metamorphosis is a generator of tales, and is one of the principles of literature itself.

The comedy of identity turns necessarily on verbal games in *Zazie.* When he is a policeman, Trouscaillon can face an "Unknown" and demand that the person produce those papers that confer identity. The phony cop's demands generate an excess that demonstrates the extraordinary implications of the very notion of identity, for Trouscaillon wants "Surname christian names date of birth place of birth social security registration number number of bank account post-office savings book rent receipt water-rate receipt gas receipt electricity receipt metro season ticket bus season ticket hire-purchase bill refrigerator brochure key ring ration books paper signed to blank permit papal bull and tutti frutti . . ." (180). The Unknown replies by pointing to a tourist bus, a reductive gesture that suffices to grant identity by showing a relation: he is Fedor Balanovitch, tour guide (and phony Russian . . .). Or Pedro, the man who has forgotten his name, can nonetheless offer an autobiography with the simple résumé that life has made him what he is. In effect, this tautology is as satisfying as "I am I" for a complete identity. Queneau's parody of the procedures of identity aims at both life and literature, at those processes of ordering by which we use language to identify things and give ourselves the impression that we live in a trustworthy world of familiar semantic categories. The comic writer knows that identity is a question of linguistic order that can be demonically disrupted. Pedro-Mephisto is there to demonstrate the disorder that results from a use of language in which names and things go their separate ways.

Zazie also has an identity provided by the disorder she foments in language. Her recurrent *mon cul* (my ass) is a name tag that is also a form of verbal aggression that respects nothing. In an interview with Marguerite Duras that has become something of an appendix to the novel, Queneau said that, in creating this heroine whom he saw as around eleven or twelve years old, he had no satirical intent; she should be taken as "normal."[7] If Zazie is normal, and in a sense she is, it is because she wants to follow the dictates of her desires with a single-mindedness that allows no dissuasion. She is the normal expression of a pleasure principle that in its total narcissism would destroy, verbally at least, anything that stands in the way of its realization.

Few would claim "normality," however, for the disparity between her age and sex, on the one hand, and her sailor's language on the other. But this comic incongruity is part of the festive impulse that puts aggression in the service of desire. Whether she wants to see the Metro, drink a coke, or find out if her uncle is a "hormosessual," Zazie employs a destructive energy that recalls Harpo Marx—though Zazie can speak, and speak she does. The high point of Queneau's linguistic potlatch comes when she tells Pedro her tale of being nearly raped by her father, this all arranged by her mother so that she could bash in his head with an ax and then take up with the butcher, who then began to eye Zazie. The comic effect resides here not only in this grotesque parody of Oedipal fantasies, but also in the relish with which Zazie delights in her gusty rendering of this bloodshed. The act of telling itself is a festive form of aggression.

Later in the novel Zazie sleeps, which might suggest that the final slug-fest and the shoot-out are dreams of her dreams. These are movie-inspired dreams of fantastic violence, for *Zazie* is another work rooted in popular culture, even if Queneau calls upon Aristotle for his epigraph. The epigraph roughly reads, "He modeled and he destroyed"; it implies that Queneau sees a certain metaphysical proposition underlying the creation of forms and their destruction. Aristotle's creator embodies forms but then destroys them, though we know that the forms are eternal. In its celebration of destruction *Zazie* is another celebration of the power of literature to disrupt those codified forms that make up the sacrosanct foundations of culture, though disruption is necessary for their renewal. Roland Barthes has spoken of the "derision" at work in *Zazie*. In our perspective it seems more appropriate to speak of Zazie's celebration of literature as the only cultural activity that can contest those cultural systems that would ossify existence in fixed forms. Just as Zazie relishes her role as enfant terrible, *Zazie* glories in disorder and the destruction of forms, including the fixed forms of the language of literature itself.

With *Zazie in the Metro* Queneau achieved best-seller success, for the novel had extraordinary appeal for a generation whose sense of humor had been refined by an absurdist vision of the world. Queneau did not allow success to interfere with his love of zany experimentation, and in his next novel he decided to explore some of the implications for fiction that Chinese thought might have. In *Les Fleurs bleues* (*Between Blue and Blue*—in the American edition, *The Blue Flowers,* 1965) he uses a parable from the Taoist sage Chuang Tzu. This parable tells that the philosopher once dreamed that he was a butterfly and, upon awaking, wondered if he might not now be a butterfly dreaming he is a philosopher. Queneau uses this parable about dream metamorphosis as a springboard for constructing a novel about the metaphysics of history. *Between Blue and Blue* uses not only a narrative structure that narrates alternate dream states, but also a Joycean circular history about eternal return. Nietzsche, *Finnegans Wake,* and the Tao are a few of the intertextual resonances that make this work one of Queneau's richest novels.

*Finnegans Wake* ends in the middle of a sentence that is completed on the first page. This is one of Joyce's ways for dramatizing Vico's vision of the cycles of history. Queneau ends *Between Blue and Blue* with his hero, the duke of Auge, atop his keep's battlements, over-looking the historical situation, which is the same scene that opens the novel during the reign of Saint Louis. The duke's opening musings, full of puns on the "historical scene," are surely an homage to Joyce's love of wordplay. Moreover, like Stephen in Joyce's *Ulysses,* the duke is sated by history: "So much history, just for a few puns and a few anachronisms. I think it's pathetic. Shan't we ever get away from it?"[8] One way to escape history is to recognize that it is all a dream. Stephen wants to awake from it, but Queneau accepts dream to shape his novel, making it the substance of history.

He has constructed his novel as a circular history composed of two series of dream episodes. One series, with the duke as hero, moves toward the historical present before returning to the beginning. The duke of Auge, much like Virginia Woolf's Orlando, appears at intervals of 175 years, going from the time of Saint Louis to the present moment set in 1964. Alternating with these "his-torical" episodes (historical because preceding the present) are the narrative sections telling about the life of Cidrolin, a Parisian living on a barge on the Seine, set in the moment of contemporary "history." Moreover, each character dreams the life of the other so that the narrative transitions from one character to another are motivated by the fact that one of them falls asleep. The narration about the duke is a dream by Cidrolin, and vice versa, at least until the novel's end when the duke arrives in Paris and takes lodging on Cidrolin's barge, the *Arch*. The characters are finally separated when an archetypical flood arrives, the duke sails away to return to his castle, and Cidrolin is last seen rowing away to parts unknown. Like Noah's before him, the duke's flood leaves him with an image of hope, for he finds that blue flowers grow from the mud that covers everything.

Cidrolin's dreams narrate the history that the duke lives, and these episodes, involving a cast of recurrent characters including a horse that talks, have a comic book quality about them, something like Astyanax, in which history is reduced to the easily remembered clichés that every schoolchild takes away from school as official history. Queneau plays with anachronisms throughout these episodes, perhaps to show that we project onto history our own present fantasies. The duke, for instance, is invited to accompany Saint Louis on a crusade, but he has no heart for "colonial wars" and turns him down. The duke is constantly set against authority and embodies a kind of pleasure-seeking principle of aggression that makes him a close kin of Zazie. When he turns down the king, the local populace disapproves of him, which in turn causes him to massacre the assembled villains and bourgeois. An aristocratic rebel, the duke joyously lives out fantasies of violence and pleasure, another Rabelaisian representative of the festive impulse.

These three motifs—cartoon images of "real" history, anachronism, and festive aggression—intertwine throughout the duke's advance through time. "Real" history establishes a chronological framework for each episode: the periods of Saint Louis, of Charles VII, the beginning of the seventeenth century, and the time of the French Revolution. Anachronism is often ironically pointed, as when the duke finds the king's police surrounding his castle walls demanding reparations for the slaughtered burghers. These police are called the CRS, recalling the Compagnie Républicaine de Sécurité that later gained such fame during the May events of 1968, but which here are the members of the Compagnie Royale de Sécurité ("Royal" rather than "Republican" security forces). Festive aggression can also be linked to real historical events, as when the duke becomes a partisan of Gilles de Rais—whose petty sins are merely to eat a few children, among other crimes against nature. One is not surprised that the duke is later a friend of that master of transgression, the Marquis de Sade.

The final historical moment, set in 1789, contains the key episode for Queneau's ironic undermining of history. Showing little interest in the Bastille or other "historical" events, the duke is now a *phil-osophe* who wants to shake the church's foundations by showing that the creation of the world did not take place four thousand years ago. He therefore selects some caves in the Périgord region (where the famous Lascaux cave is located), paints the walls with animal pictures, and shows them to his chaplain as the work of the pre-Adamite giants mentioned in the Bible. Unfortunately, the Revolution occurs, which distracts public attention from the wall paintings and allows one to conclude, against received opinion, that the Revolution, rather than weakening the church through its attack on Christianity, actually saved the church from discredit, or so the duke's chaplain reasons. To avoid the revolutionary scaffold, the duke accepts an invitation for hospitality from the count Altaviva y Altamira, a name recalling both Beaumarchais's count in his prerevolutionary *The Marriage of Figaro* and the region in Spain where other prehistoric cave paintings are found. Beaumarchais may have set forth demands for justice that history had yet to realize, but the duke created the empirical evidence for history itself. The count's name underscores Queneau's view that history, in whatever sense we mean it, may be a rather amusing contrivance.

In alternation with the duke's knockabout hunting and dueling are narrated the events, or really nonevents, that make up Cidrolin's life. This modern Parisian's life stagnates like the garbage caught by his barge in the Seine's backwaters. His days are entirely given over to repetition, to eating disgusting meals, drinking "essence of fennel," and painting over the graffiti on his fence, which, it appears until the end of the novel, are painted regularly by an unknown person. These graffiti accuse Cidrolin, falsely, of being an assassin, a charge for which he spent some time in preventive detention. It is, however, Cidrolin himself who in a compulsive act of self-accusation paints the defaming graffiti.

In this self-accusation Cidrolin differs notably from the duke of Auge, whose conduct is joyously amoral. Many of the events in Cidrolin's life are, however, doubles of what occurs in the duke's life. He sees motley crowds of international tourists who seem to be doubles of the migrating tribes that the duke views at the novel's outset. Each character has three daughters, and each takes another wife in their reciprocal dreams. One could multiply examples of this kind, though it suffices to see that they are different in their identity as the same character, which Queneau amusingly reveals finally when the two discover, on meeting each other, that they have the same name. The numerous doublings offer a kind of redundancy of possible joinings that never quite fit together, except through the dream logic that allows one to be the other and yet different.

A third character enters this dream logic and plays a crucial role when the duke arrives in Paris. Cidrolin makes the acquaintance of a camping ground guardian who is a replica of Cartesian man, since he defines himself as a "thinker" who does not dream. When the duke decides to capture the unknown graffiti painter who plagues Cidrolin, he seizes the guardian, who has recently become the concierge of a building under construction. This Cartesian reveals himself to be La Balance—or justice. He claims that he has spent his life righting wrongs and, fearing competition, has therefore been lurking about to see who has been denouncing Cidrolin. Having killed a fair number himself, he seems to get his own just desserts when the building he oversees puts an end to him by collapsing on him.

The marked differences that the three main characters present have suggested to a critic like Anne Clancier that Queneau is writing a Freudian allegory, with the id, the ego, and the superego each duly represented.[9] With the crash of the "superstructure" and the death of the exterminating superego one might see the triumph of the body or the id. The flood carries the duke back to the beginning, and with this archetypical image of renewal it seems to us that it is reasonable to speak of the triumph of the festive principal, which is always centered on the body. With some greater ingenuity one could call the flood a sign that repressive forces, in a psychoanalytic sense, have been washed away, though this interpretation must be squared with a critical irony that Queneau has inscribed throughout the novel and which seems to anticipate a Freudian reading. The novel's epigraph, for example, is from Plato, and most critics have translated it as "dreams for the dreamer." But it might also be rendered as "dreams for the interpreter of dreams," which would suggest Queneau's detached stance toward all attempts at reading dreams with a symbolic grid. Moreover, Queneau clearly parodies the Freudian attempt to set up a typology of dreams when the duke's chaplain, trying to make sense of dreams with a medieval scholastic typology, finally admits that most dreams do not mean much at all. Cidrolin also tries to explain Freudian psychoanalysis to Lalie, the upshot of which is his recognition that if one wrote down all his dreams, they would constitute a novel. And, in fact, here they do.

The question is again, then, how does one interpret these dreams? Queneau is obviously teasing the reader with a possibly circular Freudian allegory that closes in upon itself in its dream logic. These dreams are also history, but that does not promise them any great significance. Inscribed within each of the series of episodes is a comic metahistorical debate that makes light of the attempts of historiography to define the object of its science. The duke, for instance, wants his chaplain to define for him historical categories. They decide that the Council of Basel is universal history in general, whereas the duke's new cannon are an example of general history in particular. Cidrolin, his daughters, and their husbands argue about whether newsreels are history, since the news of today is the history of tomorrow. One character argues that if one had Napoleon on film, one would not need to read a book about him; for the evening news on television is history the moment it is shown, and a newsreel of Napoleon's life would be history *en directe*. Other characters demur, and hold that history only exists when it is written (an opinion also held, for example, by Levi-Strauss). This comic argument about the ontology of history provides ironic linkage with the dream parable, for if history is film, then it is a type of dream. This comic linkage is suggested not only by the novel's dream structure but by the following incident: Cidrolin and his maid Lalie go to the movies, but afterward neither can agree as to what they have seen, since each has lived his own film as a solipsistic moment of dream vision. History might exist as a filmed moment of reality, but that reality would then only be each man's private reverie.

This reduction of history to the present moment of dream is quite compatible with a cyclical view of history; moreover, it rejects any Hegelian notion of history as progress. In this cyclical view nothing exists except the present of the eternally recurring moment, which, as in *Finnegans Wake,* cannot finally be differentiated from any other moment. The archetypical flood obliterates the past as it brings back purified beginnings, but beginnings that are always here and now.

There is, perhaps, one aspect of the past in the novel, and that is found in language, for language is historical in its development. In his use of archaic forms and literary allusions Queneau may well have remembered the chapter in *Ulysses* in which Joyce writes a series of parodies of the unfolding history of styles in English literature, for literary style is another mark of the historical development of language. The presence of archaic forms of language and style is not necessarily a form of history, however; and one could argue that Queneau's linguistic play wants again to abolish history by making past language something that lives in the present. In any case, in *Between Blue and Blue* Queneau takes advantage of his "historical" progression to allude to and to parody an enormous range of past and modern works: Homer, the Bible, Charles D'Orleans, Calderon, Du Bellay, Ronsard, Shakespeare (always Hamlet), Descartes, Beaumarchais, Sade, Baudelaire, Braudel, Robbe-Grillet, to offer a few names that come to mind in this Rabelaisian fête that mixes historically marked forms of French with travesties of specific literary works. It should be noted that Queneau's play with historically marked forms of language gives the translator great freedom to invent an equivalent, and in Barbara Wright's excellent translation the reader of English finds examples of language running from Chaucer through Dryden that re-create Queneau's linguistic potlatch. This translation offers a rare example of a work that can be enjoyed as much as a re-creation as a translation.

Translation difficulties are much greater, however, for Queneau's last novel, published eight years before Queneau's death, during the tumultuous year of 1968. *Le Vol d'Icare* has been translated as *The Flight of Icarus,* but the word *vol* also allows "The Theft of Icarus," and both meanings are at work in Queneau's title. As a mythological hero Icarus flew high, only to fall when his wings were melted by the sun; as a literary archetype he has been "stolen" by many a writer, from the Ovid who gives Queneau's novel its epigraph to such moderns as W. H. Auden, Joyce, and Raymond Queneau. Ovid's verse asks where one shall look for Icarus, and the answer appears to be everywhere, including a fictional novel by Hubert Lubert contained within a (real) novel by Queneau. Or rather Icarus would be in Lubert's novel if one day a gust of wind had not blown him from that novel out into the world of Queneau's novel.

Finding his character missing Queneau's Lubert decides that his character must have been stolen. He hires a detective who notes how Pirandellian this situation is, though one could just as well see a reversal of Pirandello's famous play: in Queneau's novel the fic-

tional author, and eventually all the authors in the novel, are in
search of a character, rather than the contrary.

The search for Icarus starts badly, since the detective Morcol
spends most of his time looking for Nick Harwit, after he mis-
understands Lubert's telling him to find "mon Icare vite" (or "my
Nick Harwit" pronounced in French). This wordplay on a character's
name is matched by another when we find Icarus in a café, consorting
with the prostitute LN, letters whose French pronunciation gives
us, not a character reduced to mere initials as in Kafka, Robbe-
Grillet, or Queneau himself, but "Helen," one of the richest archetypes of Western literature. Queneau's modern beauty works on
the sidewalks, while his other archetype begins to fulfill his modern
destiny by studying mechanics.

Lubert, driven to distraction, consults a doctor whose modern
methods consist in having his patient stretch out on a sofa and tell
whatever goes through his head. Queneau's fairly systematic satire
of psychoanalysis is accompanied by a satire on the coterie of writers
that Lubert frequents. For example, Jacques, a symbolist writer,
wishes to abolish the subject matter in his current book and give
the impression of the color mauve (though his book must perforce
contain an adultery in it). Queneau's satire aims back at symbolist
writers and beyond them to his own mentor, Flaubert, who wished
in *Madame Bovary* to write a book about "nothing." Queneau's
ridicule also has a contemporary resonance, for Lubert's confrere
recalls more than a few recent modern writers who desired to write
books that demonstrate primarily their own functioning.

Morcol finds a young man resembling Icarus, but he turns out
to be a character who has escaped from Jacques's novel. (Identifying
characters is as difficult here as in any of Queneau's other novels.)
When Morcol does identify Icarus and bring him back to Lubert,
Lubert keeps him but a short time. Applying to Icarus the logic of
the belief that a character must be "true to life," the other novelists
kidnap him by claiming that, as a young citizen, he must do his
military service. Icarus gets away from them, as do their other
characters, such as the lovely Adélaïde and the symbolist Professor
Maîtretout. These two go in search of Icarus, characters in search
of a character, and a possible romance blooms. Icarus meets another
character in the "person" of a gentleman who fled his novel because
he had no desire to chop up his adulterous wife, as the novelist had

planned for him. It was not, so to speak, in his character to assassinate someone.

The archetype for the inventor, Icarus continues to make progress in mechanics by working for the automobile dealer Berrurier. There are too many women in Icarus's life, however, and he and his new friends are run off by the garage owner, especially since Berrurier's daughter is interested, too. True to character Icarus becomes interested in kite flying, but finally decides he will go back to Lubert's novel if the writer will have him back. At first Lubert refuses, then changes his mind, and arrives at the "cantharodrome" in time to see Icarus soar, rise above the clouds, and then fall. Lubert's novel "is finished," as is Queneau's, when Icarus fulfills his destiny at this "beetledrome," acting like a Greek *kantaros* (beetle) or, in French, *cerf-volant,* a word meaning both kite and a species of beetle. Aviation takes many forms.

*The Flight of Icarus* is one of Queneau's finest displays of the creative possibilities of logical paradox. For example, this work is called a novel, but it is written almost entirely in dialogue, much like a play. Do plays and novels present the same kinds of characters? Queneau's characters ask these questions about other characters when, for instance, Morcol informs Lubert that in his search for Icarus he has visited all types of writers, including novelists, historians, epic poets, and even dramatic authors. To which Lubert replies that the latter group could be of no use, since "a character in a novel can't become a character in a play."[10] Having now frequented a few literati, Morcol argues in turn that a Goncourt character could be in a novel before appearing in a play and that Manon Lescaut was in a novel before appearing in an opera (69). Lubert, however, refuses to recognize that the singing Manon could have anything in common with the one found in the novel by Abbé Prévost. They are "different" characters.

If there can be two or more Manon Lescauts, one must ask if there can be more than one Icarus. How can they, like Pedro Surplus, be the same, yet different? Or different, yet the same? These paradoxes entail that we recognize that this Icarus is the same as the one in Ovid, and yet different, since Queneau's Icarus has a past that was invented for him by Lubert (as invented by Queneau, to be sure). He was born in 1875, saw the Universal Exposition when he was fourteen, and then saw all this crossed out by the novelist. Though erased, this specifying past continues to exist, as a fictional possibility, in the pages of a novel, as the kind of negative being that entrances Saturnin in *The Bark Tree*. For the ontology of fiction grants being to every conceivable possibility, once it is imagined to exist.

In spite of Lubert's disdain for theater we know that in a sense Icarus, like Manon, is the same character as all the other versions of him, for he shares certain recurring traits that allow us to speak of an "archetype" that confers common identity. The metaphysics of identity in the case of fictional characters may appear Platonic, and this undoubtedly accounts for the fun Queneau takes in playing with these paradoxes: how does the archetype, like the Platonic "idea," come to be embodied in the particular character? Plato never resolved that problem, and Queneau is clearly amused by the conundrums posed by such a Platonic dilemma about universals when it comes to talking about literature and problems of identity.

In a different perspective Queneau is also playing with received ideas about character in fiction. In recent years, for example, with the advent of the New Novel, critics and theorists often spoke of the disappearance of character in fiction or of the decentering of subject in writing. In *The Flight of Icarus* Queneau has quite simply literalized a theoretical description. The character disappears from the novel in which he was to appear, with the result that Lubert, like Mallarmé, is left literally staring at the blank page. No writer in the twentieth century was ever less concerned than Queneau with problems of psychological portrayal in fiction, but he was also well aware of the implications of the impossible literature that many of his contemporaries demanded: a literature without characters. Whether defined as "actants" or "potentialities of discourse," to use structuralist terminology, characters are an a priori necessity for narration; and in their disappearance they necessarily reappear, even if portrayed in their flight. Icarus is the emblem of the postmodern character.

The mirror opposite of the absent character of recent theory about character is the traditional humanist view that characters should be "true to life." "Life" is a somewhat amorphous notion, but it does seem quite "true to life" for a character to prefer to exist on his own, outside of the confines of a book, where he or she can make his or her decisions about "life." What normal person "in life" would want to murder his spouse, however adulterous she may have been, merely because an egomanical writer, seeking fame and fortune, wanted him to do so? Queneau's characters are "true to life," or at least to that selected portion of our ordinary experience, in the everyday world, in which people do not wish to murder other people and prefer to make their own decisions. Of course, making decisions entails taking risks, of trying sometimes to fly on one's own wings, and if a person crashes to the ground in failure, then we might be tempted to say that (real) person was an Icarus. Characters do have a curious way of existing outside of books.

Queneau's last novel delights in those paradoxes about being and nonbeing that, as we noted, his would-be writer Saturnin posed for readers thirty-five years earlier in *The Bark Tree.* Perhaps *The Flight of Icarus* is the book Saturnin might have written, if he had had Queneau's skeptical but festive sense of the limits of theoretical thought. For Queneau, fiction was constantly the corrective that liberated one from the systematic imagination by showing the possibilities of excess contained therein. In parody and sometimes festive derision literature can literalize any proposition about the world and show its absurd implications. It is fitting that Queneau's final novel should have been a work about literature, for his skeptical mind would give no final assent to any proposition, not even to the proposition that literature is the skeptic's final refuge. With his paradoxes about identity, character, and fictive being, Queneau showed that he was an inheritor of that Renaissance that counted among its greatest achievements not only the carnivalesque work of Rabelais, but also the dialectical skepticism of a Montaigne.

# Chapter Six
# Conclusion

Having suggested some of the excitement that can be generated by following Queneau's creative itinerary, I shall now offer in conclusion a résumé of what Queneau's legacy appears to be, a few years after his death. His literary legacy is bound up with two forms of practice: the practice of fiction as a self-reflexive intellectual comedy and the practice of language as a parodistic form of transgression. First, with regard to the fiction, it seems accurate to claim that Queneau's novels are nearly always impregnated with a hyperbolic, but ironic, awareness of their status as a literary construct. Queneau uses many devices for inscribing this awareness within the individual work; what is crucial is that the reader is never allowed to forget that, at every point in the novel, a critical mind is constantly on display, showing the arbitrary play that underlies choices of events and characters, style and diction. Fabulation is a construct, and it often seems that every sentence in Queneau proclaims its participation in a game that could have been played by other rules.

A few examples will suffice to recall some of Queneau's ironic techniques for creating self-reflexivity. In *The Bark Tree,* a nearly manifestolike attack on realist fiction, Queneau endows the novel with a surrogate narrator who acts as a kind of persona or fictional mask tying together the circular movement of a novel that ends where it begins after the characters decide to erase the text. In *Les Enfants du Limon* the novel involutes upon itself when Raymond Queneau becomes a character to accept the gift of the crank encyclopedia that generated the novel in the first place. Negative self-reflexivity occurs in *Pierrot* when the hero imagines what a novel his adventures could have made, but did not—except in the novel that Queneau wrote. Whether it be with characters who dream each other's adventures, as in *Between Blue and Blue,* or with characters who are "real" characters from fictional books, as in *The Flight of Icarus,* Queneau's novels never passively enact mimesis with a feigned blindness about their status as fictions. One literary game is of course to pretend that a novel is not a novel; but Queneau prefers to write works that are lucid, often comically lucid, about their own nature, and which demand a constant reflection on the nature of literature and the demands it may make upon the reader.

This ironic lucidity about the status of fiction is part of the intellectual comedies that Queneau stages through his festive parody of other forms of representation. By "forms of representation" one should understand all those cultural forms—literature, philosophy, history, science, religion—that purport to order reality and to communicate this order through transmissible codes. Queneau often deforms these codes of representation in order to use them as the substance of his fictions. This deformation is part of the desacralization that Queneau's parody undertakes. It is the work of the liberated skeptical mind that delights in showing the limits of representation, metaphysics, anthropological concepts, literary forms, and religious beliefs. Through incongruous juxtapositions, absurd if logical literalizations, and carnivalesque language, Queneau demonstrates the limits of the intellect by his travesties of all representations that might limit our experience of the world and its heterogeneous orders.

This respect of heterogeneity, this refusal of monist systematizing, is part of a modern rationalism that recognizes that there are as many systems, as many languages for describing the world, as there are minds capable of creating persuasive orders of representation. In this respect Queneau is a prototypically modern rationalist, not unlike his near contemporary, the Austrian philosopher Ludwig Wittgenstein. This comparison may at first seem surprising, but it is useful on many counts, especially to show that Queneau shared, in his novels and his essays, many of the preoccupations of a form of rationalism that is not often accepted in France. Like Wittgenstein, Queneau was concerned with the limits of language and saw it, as Wittgenstein said about mathematics, as a great motley that could not be reduced to a single order of explanation. Both were interested in mathematics and what it could and could not say about the world; and they had a comparable interest in Freud. And like Wittgenstein, who saw in language multiple forms of games that had no common essence, Queneau had a ludic mind that saw in game metaphors a way of viewing the multiple forms of representation that offer access to reality. For Wittgenstein the world is informed by an indefinite number of language games; and Queneau's work is a great demonstration that language is a ludic field offering indefinite possibilities for articulating the real. The Wittgenstein of *The Philosophical Investigations* wrote philosophy that tried to demystify the hold that misuse of language might have on us.[1] The Queneau of the novels desacralizes the systems that have mystified us with their claims to unify the world. And both these rationalist skeptics probably believed that our most essential concerns were not accessible to any language.

Queneau's play with forms of representation, from Parmenides and Plato through Freud, Mauss, and the New Novel, suggest his skeptical sense of the limits of any attempt to seize the real. Is it, then, a paradox that many of Queneau's best readers find in his work a representation of a certain French social reality that is unsurpassed in modern fiction? Perhaps no writer, with the possible exception of Céline, has so well defined the conditions of banality that make up the average everydayness of the French lower–middle class; and metonymically, the essential banality of the world itself. Of course, Queneau's petty bourgeois world, in which one's highest aspiration is an aperitif and a good sauce, provides the grid of messy experience for which Einstein and Freud, Hegel and Heidegger, are called to offer an adequate account. Behind this opposition stands the festive demands of the carnival spirit, which, in parody and travesty, obliges the pretensions of high or sacred culture to account for the material body.

Festive play with its affirmation of innocence characterizes both the novels and the poems, and Queneau's transgressive use of language is central to both bodies of work. The poet Alain Bosquet held that Queneau is one of the great French poets of the twentieth century because in his poems he made language explode, but the same judgment would also apply to Queneau's novels.[2] In this respect his legacy is to have left a model for the creation of festive strategies, using spoken French and the resources of extraordinary erudition, for the transgression of the received codes of literary French and the representations encoded therein. Transgression involves the self-conscious violation, often through capricious spelling, oral syntax, neologisms, or incongruous *mots savants,* of a recognized norm. "Doukipudontan"—"How can they stink so much"—is the perfumed Gabriel's first sentence in *Zazie;* and with this arbitrary representation of the normal, equally arbitrary spelling of popular language, an entire festive universe, as well as the fallen reality of stinking crowds, is condensed into one assault upon the norms of codified language.

This kind of transgression is invariably funny, not only because of its bizarre appearance, but because it takes place in a context in which it stands opposed to representations of the world by Sartre and Shakespeare, not to mention the Aristotle whose Greek gives *Zazie* its title page's look of profound erudition. Queneau's most successful transgression against codified norms always occurs in the context of his self-reflexive comedies. When, for example, the poet of "Si tu t'imagines" tells the young damsel who counts on exploiting her beauty forever, "ce que tu te goures"—roughly "you're really wrong, kid"—the transgression is not simply a matter of writing slangy French. It involves a violation of the poetic norms of expression that have evolved during the history of French poetry, that is, since Ronsard first used the Horatian theme of carpe diem in the Renaissance. This is another rich example of Queneau's parody. It transgresses the received order of poetic representation while at the same time it offers an inverted affirmation of that neoclassical tradition of which Queneau was a festive defender. For in parody also lies renewal of the tradition.

I conclude this study with no great claim for Queneau's place in the tradition, since such a claim would be inconsonant with a body of work that finds Heraclitean permanence only in the permanent intransience of the ten thousand things. For the ephemeral time known as our lifetime, however, we expect to see Queneau's poems and novels increasingly evaluated as one of the most interesting bodies of work of modern French and also world literature. I would expect to see that, after such writers as Ionesco, Robbe-Grillet, Calvino, and Perec, more writers and readers will be attracted to Queneau's work and its defense of literature's necessity as our only cultural institution that exists as the playful and liberating negation of all other institutions. Many of the functions of literature, its uses for knowledge, historical identity, or moral initiation, can be fulfilled by other cultural forms. But Queneau's example shows that nothing can replace literature as the festive potlatch that contests as it renews our cultural possibilities. This defense and illustration of literature could well be Queneau's perduring legacy.

# Notes and References

*Chapter One*

1. *Raymond Queneau plus intime* (Paris, 1978), 14; catalog of an exhibition held at the Bibliothèque nationale.
2. This and much other information comes from the useful chronology that André Blavier compiled for the special issue of *Europe*, June–July 1983, 130–48.
3. For a good formulation of these points see Italo Calvino's introduction to Queneau's work in *Les Amis de Valentin Brû*, no. 15 (1981):13–15.
4. In the last essays printed in *Le Voyage en Grèce* (Paris, 1973).
5. This is the story, for example, in "Connaissez-vous le chinook," in *Bâtons, chiffres et lettres* (Paris, 1965) 59.
6. This is the later story in "Errata," in *Le Voyage en Grèce*, 220.
7. "Philosophes et voyous," *Les Temps modernes*, January 1951, 1193.
8. Blavier, in *Europe*, 137.
9. This is developed in "Les mathématiques dans la classification des sciences," in *Bords* (Paris, 1963), 123–30.
10. "Présentation de l'*Encyclopédie*," in *Bords*, 104. Translations throughout, unless otherwise noted, are mine.
11. See Queneau's "David Hilbert," in *Die Grossen der Weltgeschichte* (Zurich: Kindler Verlag, 1970), 501–19. This essay is available only in this German text.
12. Descriptions of early sessions of Oulipo are found in Jacques Bens, *Oulipo 1960–1963* (Paris, 1982). I have also based my description on personal participation in a public session.

*Chapter Two*

1. *Vlaminck ou le vertige de la matière* (Geneva, 1949).
2. *L'Instant fatal* and *Les Ziaux* (Paris, 1966), 111.
3. "Textes surréalistes," *Révolution surréaliste*, no. 11 (1928):13.
4. This line from "Le bon usage des maladies," in *L'Instant fatal* (89), finds an echo in Queneau's work years later in "Le boulanger sans complexe" of *Fendre les flots* in which the psychoanalyst navigates on a sewer and fishes up rusting cans that he can attribute to dreams. Note also that Queneau changes *Traumdeutung* to *Bedeutung*, "interpretation" to "meaning," but the reference can only be to Freud.
5. *Chêne et chien* and *Petite cosmogonie portative* (Paris, 1969), 31.

6. Noël Arnaud, "Mais où est donc passé *Chêne et chien?*," *Temps mêlés*, no. 150 + 17–18–19 (1983):21.

7. "Sixième émission," *Les Amis de Valentin Brû*, no. 8 (1979).

8. Wladimir Krysinski, "La voix des métaphores," *L'Herne*, special Queneau issue (1975):208.

9. Claude Debon-Tournadre, "Présence d' Apollinaire dans l'oeuvre de Raymond Queneau," *Revue d'Histoire littéraire de la France*, January–February 1981, 75–92.

10. Jacques Guicharnard, *Raymond Queneau* (New York, 1965), 29.

11. *Exercises in Style*, trans. Barbara Wright (New York, 1981), 23.

*Chapter Three*

1. *Taschenkosmogonie*, trans. Ludwig Harig (Wiesbaden, 1963), 7.

2. *Petite cosmogonie portative* (Paris, 1969). This version differs slightly from the first edition. Queneau has removed some argot and obscenity. The first edition is currently available, however, in the bilingual *Piccola Cosmogonia portatile*, trans. Sergio Solmi (Turin:Einaudi, 1982). This translation also has a good study of the work by Italo Calvino.

3. Jean Rostand, "Raymond Queneau et la cosmogonie," *Critique*, June 1951, 483–91.

4. *Le Chien à la Mandoline* (Paris, 1965), 20. This expanded edition also contains his *Sonnets*.

5. Queneau explicitly corrects Hegel in this collection's sonnet "Encore une fois les hibous"—"Owls Again"—by noting that owls fly only at night (198).

6. *Courir les rues, Battre la campagne, Fendre les flots* (Paris, 1980), 91; references to these three collections refer to this one-volume edition in Gallimard's Collection Poésie.

7. Marcel Granet, *La Pensée chinoise* (Paris: Albin Michel, 1968), 272.

8. James J. Y. Liu, "Literary Qualities of the Lyric (Tz'u)," in *Studies in Chinese Literary Genres*, ed. Cyril Birch (Berkeley: University of California Press, 1974), 149.

9. *Morale élémentaire* (Paris, 1975), 12.

10. Ezra Pound, *ABC of Reading* (New York, 1960), 32.

*Chapter Four*

1. Many critics have made much of the numerological motivation that Queneau wanted to provide for the structure of *The Bark Tree*. Little of this motivation is evident, however, in the actual experience of reading the novel. His "Technique du roman" in *Bâtons, chiffres et lettres* gives a good explanation of how he used number schemes in his attempt to rescue novelistic form from the suspicion that it is arbitrary and gratuitous.

2. *The Bark Tree,* trans. Barbara Wright (New York, 1971), 25.

3. Jacob's comparison is specifically to *The Possessed,* in *L'Herne,* 214.

4. Nicolas Hewitt, "History in *Les Enfants du Limon:* Encyclopaedists and 'flaneurs,' " *Prospice,* no. 8 (1978):22–35.

5. Letters reprinted in *Les Amis de Valentin Brû,* no. 19 (1982):9–20.

6. *Pierrot mon ami* (Paris, n.d.), 211.

7. Albert Camus, "Pierrot mon ami," in *Essais* (Paris: Gallimard, 1965), 1928–30; translated by Douglas Kerr in *Prospice,* no. 8 (1978):36.

8. Gaëton Picon, "Queneau plutôt à part," *L'Herne,* no. 29 (1975):72.

9. *Loin de Rueil* (Paris, n.d.), 41.

## Chapter Five

1. Gilbert Pestureau, "Les techniques anglo-saxonnes et l'art romanesque de Raymond Queneau," *Europe,* June–July 1983, 112.

2. *We Always Treat Women Too Well,* trans. Barbara Wright (New York, 1981), 4–6.

3. *Les oeuvres complètes de Sally Mara* (Paris, 1962), 17.

4. *The Sunday of Life,* trans. Barbara Wright (New York, 1977), unnumbered first page.

5. Roland Barthes, "Zazie et la littérature," in *Essais critiques* (Paris, 1964), 126.

6. *Zazie in the Metro,* trans. Barbara Wright (New York, 1982), 100.

7. "UNEURAVEK: A Conversation with Marguerite Duras," in *Prospice,* 53.

8. *Between Blue and Blue,* trans. Barbara Wright (London, 1967), 7.

9. Anne Clancier, "Le Manuel du parfait analysé," *L'Arc,* no. 28 (1966):33–40.

10. *The Flight of Icarus,* trans. Barbara Wright (New York, 1973), 68.

## Chapter Six

1. Ludwig Wittgenstein, *Philosophical Investigations,* trans. G. E. M. Anscombe (New York: Macmillan, 1953).

2. Alain Bosquet, "Le rire jaune et noir de Queneau," *Magazine littéraire,* no. 94 (1974):20.

# Selected Bibliography

PRIMARY SOURCES

1. Fiction

*Le Chiendent.* Paris: Gallimard, 1933. Translated by Barbara Wright as *The Bark Tree.* London: Calder and Boyars, 1968; New York: New Directions, 1971.

*Contes et Propos.* Paris: Gallimard, 1981. This volume publishes nearly all the short pieces of fiction that Queneau wrote.

*Les Derniers Jours.* Paris: Gallimard, 1936.

*Le Dimanche de la vie.* Paris: Gallimard, 1952. Translated by Barbara Wright as *The Sunday of Life.* London: Calder, 1976; New York: New Directions, 1977.

*Les Enfants du Limon.* Paris: Gallimard, 1938.

*Exercises de style.* Paris: Gallimard, 1947. Translated by Barbara Wright as *Exercises in Style.* London: Gaberbocchus, 1958; New York: New Directions, 1981.

*Les Fleurs bleues.* Paris: Gallimard, 1965. Translated by Barbara Wright as *Between Blue and Blue.* London: Bodley Head, 1967. Published in the United States as *The Blue Flowers.* New York: Atheneum, 1967.

*Gueule de Pierre.* Paris: Gallimard, 1934.

*Journal intime.* Paris: Editions du Scorpion, 1950. Published under the pseudonym of Sally Mara.

*Loin de Rueil.* Paris: Gallimard, 1944. Translated by J. J. Kaplan as *The Skin of Dreams.* New York: New Directions, 1948.

*Odile.* Paris: Gallimard, 1937.

*Les Oeuvres complètes de Sally Mara.* Paris: Gallimard, 1962.

*On est toujours trop bon avec les femmes.* Paris: Editions du Scorpion, 1947. Published under the pseudonym of Sally Mara. Translated by Barbara Wright as *We Always Treat Women Too Well.* London: John Calder, 1981; New York: New Directions, 1981.

*Pierrot mon ami.* Paris: Gallimard, 1942. Translated by J. Maclaren-Ross as *Pierrot.* London: John Lehmann, 1950.

*Un Rude Hiver.* Paris: Gallimard, 1939. Translated by Betty Askwith as *A Hard Winter.* London: John Lehmann, 1948.

*Saint Glinglin.* Paris: Gallimard, 1948.

*Les Temps mêlés (Gueule de Pierre II).* Paris: Gallimard, 1941.

*Le Vol d'Icare.* Paris: Gallimard, 1968. Translated by Barbara Wright as *The Flight of Icarus.* London: Calder & Boyars, 1973; New York: New Directions, 1973.

*Zazie dans le métro.* Paris: Gallimard, 1959. Translated by Barbara Wright as *Zazie in the Metro.* London: Bodley Head, 1960; New York, Harper & Bros., 1960.

2. Poems

*Battre la campagne.* Paris: Gallimard, 1968.

*Bucoliques.* Paris: Gallimard, 1947.

*Cent mille milliards de poèms.* Paris: Gallimard, 1961. Translated by John Crombie as *One Hundred Million Million Poems.* Paris: Kickshaws, 1983.

*Chêne et chien.* Paris: Denoël, 1937.

*Le Chien à la mandoline.* Paris: Verviers, Temps mêlés, 1958. An augmented version, including the *Sonnets,* was published in Paris by Gallimard in 1965.

*Courir les rues.* Paris: Gallimard, 1967.

*Fendre les flots.* Paris: Gallimard, 1969.

*L'Instant fatal.* Paris: Aux Nourritures Terrestres, 1946. The first revised edition was published in Paris by Gallimard in 1948.

*Morale élémentaire.* Paris: Gallimard, 1975.

*Petite cosmogonie portative.* Paris: Gallimard, 1950. A slightly revised edition was published in Paris by Gallimard in 1969.

*Si tu t'imagines.* Paris: Gallimard, 1951. This contains largely previously published work.

*Sonnets.* Paris: Editions Hautefeuille, 1958. Included in the 1965 edition of *Le Chien à la mandoline.*

*Les Ziaux.* Paris: Gallimard, 1943.

3. Other Writings

*Bâtons, chiffres et lettres.* Paris: Gallimard, 1950. Revised edition in 1965.

*Bords: Mathématiciens, précurseurs, encyclopédistes.* Paris: Editions Hermann, 1963.

*Entretiens avec George Charbonnier.* Paris: Gallimard, 1962.

*Une Histoire modèle.* Paris: Gallimard, 1966.

"Philosophes et voyous." *Les Temps modernes,* no. 63 (January 1951):1193–1205.

"Premières confrontations avec Hegel." *Critique,* nos. 195–96 (August–September 1963):694–700.

"Récit de rêve." *La Révolution surréaliste,* no. 3 (April 1925):5.

"Texte surréaliste." *La Révolution surréaliste,* no. 5 (October 1925):3–4.

*Vlaminck ou le vertige de la matière.* Geneva: Skira, 1949.

*Le Voyage en Grèce.* Paris: Gallimard, 1973.

## SECONDARY SOURCES

### 1. Bibliographies

**Hillen, Wolfgang.** *Bibliographie des études sur l'homme et son oeuvre.* Cologne: Gemini, 1981. The most complete bibliography of critical studies and journalism devoted to Queneau's work.

**Rameil, Claude.** In *Les Amis de Valentin Brû,* no. 23 (1983). A remarkably complete bibliography of the writings of Queneau.

It should also be noted that Gallimard, in its Collection Idées, has published two collective anthologies of work by Oulipo, with much by and about Queneau: *La Littérature potentielle* (1973) and *Atlas de littérature potentielle* (1981).

### 2. Books

**Baligand, Renée A.** *Les Poèmes de Raymond Queneau.* Montreal: Didier, 1972. A good study of Queneau's rhetorical techniques using modern linguistic concepts.

**Bens, Jacques.** *Oulipo 1960–1963.* Paris: Christian Bourgois, 1980. Often amusing descriptions of Oulipo sessions.

————*Queneau.* Paris: Gallimard, Collection Bibliothèque Idéale, 1962. Still useful introduction to main themes, with excerpts from Queneau's work and from critics.

**Bergens, Andrée.** *Raymond Queneau.* Geneva: Droz, 1963. A general thematic study that is perhaps most useful on Queneau's view of the absurd. Recommended for beginning readers.

**Dauphin, Jean-Pierre,** ed. *Raymond Queneau plus intime.* Paris: Gallimard, 1978. Catalog of an exhibition at the Bibliothèque nationale. Closest thing to a biography that exists.

**Gayot, Paul.** *Raymond Queneau.* Paris: Editions Universitaires, 1967. A witty work dealing primarily with history and with the various circular shapes of the novels.

**Guicharnaud, Jacques.** *Raymond Queneau.* New York: Columbia University Press, 1965. A pamphlet-length study that provides a general introduction in English.

**Kogan, Vivian.** *The Flowers of Fiction: Time and Space in Raymond Queneau's Les Fleurs bleues.* Lexington, Ky.: French Forum, 1982. A somewhat overblown attempt at poststructuralism that nonetheless offers an original approach to the novel.

**Queval, Jean.** *Essai sur Raymond Queneau.* Paris: Seghers, 1960. Somewhat outdated, but important as first study to set up some of the categories for understanding Queneau's work.

Redfern, W.D. *Queneau: Zazie dans le metro.* London: Grant & Cutler, 1980. A critical guide to the novel that has much useful information. Written for students.

Simonnet, Claude. *Queneau déchiffré (Notes sur "le Chiendent").* Paris: Julliard, 1962. The best introduction to Queneau's literary universe, with an excellent discussion of *The Bark Tree,* using Queneau's own critical concepts to elucidate this novel and Queneau's work in general.

3. Special Issues of Periodicals

*L'Arc,* no. 28 (February 1966). Several good studies.

*Dossiers du Collège de Pataphysique,* no. 20 (July 1962).

*Europe,* nos. 650–51 (June–July 1983). Some excellent studies, with a chronology and bibliography by André Blavier.

*L'Herne,* no. 29 (December 1975). A large collection of studies, letters, *inédits.*

*Magazine littéraire,* no. 94 (November 1974).

*Prospice,* no. 8 (1978). Useful for the English public, with a few translations and some critical studies.

*Temps mêlés,* nos. 50–52 (September 1961).

4. Queneau Journals

*Les Amis de Valentin Brû.* Published by the association of the same name and edited by Claude Rameil (56, rue Carnot, 92300 Levallois-Perret, France). Devoted to the life and work of Queneau.

*Temps mêlés—Documents Queneau.* Edited by André Blavier (23, place du Général Jacques, 4800, Verviers, Belgium). Since 1978 devoted exclusively to Queneau.

5. Articles

Barthes, Roland. "Zazie et la littérature." In *Essais critiques,* 125–31. Paris: Seuil, 1964. With his usual intelligence Barthes sees Queneau as exemplary of the contradictions of the modern writer. Dazzling, if probably wrong.

Boyer, Regis. "Mots et jeux de mots chez Prévert, Queneau, Vian, Ionesco." *Studia Neophilologica,* no. 2 (1968):317–58. Helpful typology of wordplay in these writers.

Brée, Germaine, and Guiton, Margaret. "Fly in the Ointment." In *An Age of Fiction: The French Novel from Gide to Camus,* 169–79. New Brunswick, N.J.: Rutgers University Press, 1957. Good introduction in English to Queneau's early fiction.

Debon-Tournadre, Claude. "Présence d'Apollinaire dans l'oeuvre de Queneau." *Revue d'Histoire littéraire de la France* 81, no. 1 (January–February 1981):75–92. Throws much light on Queneau's intertextual play.

**Esslin, Martin.** "Raymond Queneau." In *The Novelist as Philosopher: Studies in French Fiction 1935–60,* edited by John Cruickshank, 79–101. London: Oxford University Press, 1962. High level analysis of philosophical themes in Queneau's work.

**Kojève, Alexandre.** "Les romans de la sagesse." *Critique,* no. 60 (1952):387–97. A post-Hegelian reading of Queneau.

**Mercier, Vivian.** "Raymond Queneau: The Creator as Destroyer." In *The New Novel from Queneau to Pinget,* 43–103. New York: Farrar, Straus & Giroux, 1971. First sytematic attempt to link Queneau to the generation of writers to follow him.

**Rostand, Jean.** "Queneau et la cosmogonie." *Critique,* no. 49 (1951):483–91. A biologist looks at Queneau's poetry on evolution. Dated, but interesting for how Queneau was using then contemporary science.

**Simonnet, Claude.** "La Parodie et le thème de 'Hamlet' chez Raymond Queneau." *Les Lettres nouvelles,* no. 34 (1947):16–23. An early study of one of the most important leitmotivs in Queneau's work.

# Index